Our Endangered Parks

What You Can Do to Protect Our National Heritage

❖

National Parks and Conservation Association

With p

Foghorn
Press
BOOKS BUILDING COMMUNITY.

0-935701-84-2

51095

9 780935 701845

Copyright © 1994
by National Parks and Conservation Association

Our Endangered Parks

All rights reserved. This book may not be reproduced in full or in part without the written permission of the publisher, except for use by a reviewer in the context of a review. Inquiries and excerpt requests should be addressed to:

Foghorn Press
555 DeHaro Street #220
San Francisco, CA 94107
415-241-9550

Foghorn Press titles are distributed to the book trade by Publishers Group West, Emeryville, California. To contact your local sales representative, call 1-800-788-3123.

To order individual books, please call Foghorn Press at 1-800-FOGHORN (364-4676).

Foghorn Press is committed to preservation of the environment. All Foghorn Press outdoors titles are printed on the California standard for recycled paper, which is 50% recycled paper and 10% post-consumer waste.

Printed in the United States of America.

Our Endangered Parks

What You Can Do to Protect Our National Heritage

❖

National Parks and Conservation Association

With profiles by Jeffrey Davis

Foghorn Press

BOOKS BUILDING COMMUNITY.

Credits

Managing Editor—*Howard Rabinowitz*
Editors—*Samantha Trautman, Ann-Marie Brown*
Layout & Design—*Michele Thomas, Ann-Marie Brown*
Cover Illustration—*I. Magnus*
Chapter Art—*Ron Blalock*

Photo Credits
page 12—*Laurence Parent*
page 20—*Jeff Henry*
page 59—*Kit Miller*
page 91—*George Wuerthner*
page 117—*Page Chichester*
page 145—*Russ Butcher*
page 159—*Coby Jordan*
page 188—*Patrick Short*

The profiles of park advocates which appear throughout the book were written by Jeff Davis. Jeff is a former editor of *Mother Jones* magazine and a freelance writer whose work has appeared in *The New York Times Magazine, Outside, Mother Jones* and other publications.

The research, writing and review of the book were accomplished by the following NPCA staff: Laura Loomis, David Simon, Tom St. Hilaire, Libby Fayad, Terri Martin, Bruce Craig, Jennifer Seher, Kathy Westra and Bill Chandler.

Editorial assistance was provided by Sue Dodge, Linda Rancourt, Beth Hedstrom, Laura McCarty of *National Parks* magazine and Paul Merrion. Foghorn Press's Howard Rabinowitz contributed material and shaped the individual chapters into a cohesive whole.

Special thanks to Bob Aegerter of the Mount Rainier National Park Association who drafted the chapter on forming a park advocacy group. We are also grateful to John Gingles of the National Park Service, Christine Shaver of the Environmental Defense Fund and William J. Lockhart, Professor of Law, University of Utah, who provided insightful comments on specific chapters.

Most importantly, we want to thank the hundreds of park advocates throughout the country who were the inspiration for this effort.

Preface

The National Parks and Conservation Association has successfully fought many park protection battles but now is looking more to local citizens to lead the way. Our park activist network unites NPCA members, ParkWatchers, and park advocacy groups to build a large and diverse corps of grassroots activists.

As part of its 75th anniversary celebration, NPCA has produced *Our Endangered Parks*, a manual providing the tools citizens need to bring about positive change for parks at the grassroots level.

Parks are political creations that are physically bound to greater ecosystems and emotionally tied to human events, yet their boundaries are crafted by the political whims of the time. A jumble of governmental bodies, as well as private property owners, vie for control of park resources. But what is the public's role in protecting park resources? Given the myriad players involved, can an individual make a difference? Conservationist Aldo Leopold said, "We abuse the land because we regard it as a commodity belonging to us. When we see the land as a community to which we belong, we may begin to use it with love and respect."

A tug-of-war exists between those who see parks as potential revenue sources, and those who share the view of the National Park Service's original enabling legislation, which states that parks must be preserved unimpaired for future generations. These opposing views are at the core of the struggle for park protection. Park advocates must educate themselves and the public on the issues determining this debate. They must speak out on behalf of the land. They must view the decision-making processes involved in national park issues as part of a larger political process, with both national and local players, and organize our communities at the grassroots level to bring clout to city, county, state and federal legislatures.

Park advocates must hold elected officials and administrative appointees accountable. But most of all, they must follow Leopold's charge to change our view of the land and use his words as a clarion call to action in developing a strong base of support for national park issues. To make a difference in protecting park resources, advocates must bring together various constituencies with an interest in protecting these lands and forge a commitment to future generations. They must build a park community. Only then will the diverse cultural and natural elements that make up our parks fully integrate themselves as part of America's heritage.

Table of Contents

I. Parks in Peril—What You Can Do

II. Parks Issues, Park Answers

III. Understanding Park Policy

IV. Appendices & Index

Chapter 1

Parks in Peril

Something will have gone out of us as a people if we ever let the remaining wilderness be destroyed... Without any remaining wilderness, we are committed wholly, without chance of even momentary reflection and rest, to a headlong drive into our technological termite-life, the Brave New World of a completely man-controlled environment.

Wallace Stegner

PARKS IN PERIL

It has been called "the best idea America ever had." In 1872, Congress established the first national park, Yellowstone, with a vision: to preserve the natural wonder of the land for the enjoyment of all Americans. This vision has guided the growth of the National Park System from 7.5 million acres in 1916, when Woodrow Wilson signed legislation to form the National Park Service, to its current 80.1 million acres—roughly 3.5 percent of the United States. More than 120 nations around the world have emulated the American vision by protecting their own national parklands.

All told, today's National Park System encompasses 367 national parks, preserves, monuments, historic sites, seashores, rivers and recreation areas across every American state except Delaware. Each park contains an irreplaceable treasure, be it an ecosystem rich in native plant and wildlife, an awe-inspiring landscape, a pristine seashore, a remnant of a vanished culture, or a battlefield where American history was written in blood.

No matter where you live, you are probably within a day's drive of a national park, and even closer to a state, county or local park. And your park is in peril. What are the threats facing it? Below are some notable examples:

•New York's Statue of Liberty National Monument

Recently, heavy visitation has forced the Park Service to hire a full-time employee to scrape off the more than 600 pounds of chewing gum left on Ellis Island's benches, walls and railings.

•Virginia's Shenandoah National Park

The air over Shenandoah contains the highest level of sulfur dioxide pollution over any American park, which has led to acid rain threatening the park's forests, lakes and streams. Despite protest from the National Park Service, 20 new power plants which are likely to emit sulfur dioxide have received permits to operate from Virginia since 1986. Twelve other plants are under review.

•Minnesota's St. Croix National Scenic Waterway

Construction projects and agricultural development around this and Wisconsin's Lower St. Croix Waterway have caused steep ravines to erode and led to the deposit of sediment and heavy metal pollutants in the river. High levels of pesticides and mercury have been found in native fish.

•North Dakota's Theodore Roosevelt National Park

Industrial developers hope to drill the 1.3 million acres of badlands surrounding Theodore Roosevelt National Park for oil and natural gas, and the U.S. Forest Service has announced plans to lease them the land. Currently there are 20 working drilling sites within two miles of the park's borders.

•Tennessee's Great Smoky Mountains National Park

In 1992 alone, visitors drove 3.6 million cars through the Great Smoky Mountains. Auto emissions have contributed to air pollution, reducing visibility within the park by 15 miles over the past 30 years and damaging 70 native plant species.

•Florida's Everglades National Park

The construction of canals, levees and water-control systems north and east of the park has drastically altered the natural seasonal flows of park waters, damaging the area's delicate eco-system. Several species of birds are near extinction. Chemical and nutrient pollution from upstream agriculture have ravaged select fish and shrimp populations.

•California's Joshua Tree National Monument

Developers propose building the world's largest solid waste dump 8,000 feet from Joshua Tree's border. Trains and dumptrucks will haul 20,000 tons of trash daily from Southern

California cities and counties alongside the park for 115 years. The landfill would attract large numbers of scavenging ravens, potentially deadly to the park's population of endangered desert tortoises.

Development poses a grave threat to park boundaries and the quality of the water and air within them. The spectacular vistas for which many parks, such as the Grand Canyon and Shenandoah, are renowned, are frequently smog-shrouded. Acid rain is corroding national monuments and memorials. Contaminated runoff from agricultural, ranching and residential development are polluting what should be pristine park waterways.

The extent of the damage from many of these threats is not fully appreciated because of the inadequacy of Park Service research programs. Although research and monitoring should be an essential component of park management, currently NPS only devotes two percent of its budget and three percent of its staff to research.

The National Park System faces a backlog of resource management and protection projects totaling more than $500 million and growing. The bill for repairs necessary to maintain park infrastructure—sewer systems, administrative facilities, visitor centers and employee housing—is estimated to be more than $2.2 billion.

We may be "loving our parks" to death. Each year, visitation to parks has been increasing by three percent. By the year 2000, more than 350 million visitors are expected annually at national parks. That number could reach half a billion a decade later. Unless parks start managing the numbers of visitors allowed and their recreational activities, over-visitation will continue to strain and degrade park resources.

Even though visitation is at an all-time high, lack of adequate funding means parks are cutting back on what they can offer visitors. Throughout the system, interpretive programs are being cut, campgrounds are being closed and trails are being neglected.

The human resources of the parks—park rangers and resource managers—have been stressed along with park resources over the past decade. In the early 1980s there was one ranger

Pollution from upstream development threatens pristine park waters, such as Chickasaw National Recreation Area's Travertine Creek.

for every 59,432 recreational visitors to national parks; in 1992, the ratio stood at one ranger for every 80,204 visitors. The National Park Service is suffering from the same problems affecting the government as a whole—including an inability to provide salaries and benefits that make it competitive with the private sector. For the first time in its history, the Park Service is having a difficult time recruiting and retaining qualified individuals in the 1990s.

The list goes on. While in principle it is the National Park Service's mandate to preserve national parks for their continued enjoyment by future generations, in reality the organization's bureaucracy and chronic underfunding have left it unable to address the problems facing our parks today, let alone to serve as an all-purpose watchdog for threats that could undermine parks tomorrow.

Today, the responsibility falls to the American public to become actively involved in the fate of our parks. If the crown jewels of America's natural and cultural legacy are to withstand the many forces threatening them, it will not only require a renewed recognition of their value by American citizens, it will also require people's active involvement in their preservation.

What is a "Park Advocate"?

Throughout this book, you'll find profiles of park advocates, people like Dr. Liane Russell, an environmental activist who has fought to defend Tennessee's wilderness areas since the 1940s (pg. 124)...Duane Pierson, a scientist and novelist who has helped his Maine-based citizens group, Friends of Acadia, to become an integral part of Acadia National Park's planning process (pg. 150)...Anne Wieland, a schoolteacher and volunteer for Kachemak Bay Citizens Coalition whose decade-long lobbying efforts contributed to the purchase of crucial native and mining inholdings in Alaska's Kachemak Bay State Park (pg. 96)... and Dan Trevisani, a firefighter from Utica, New York who pushed for and publicized a March for Parks event that raised much needed funds for his ailing local park system (pg. 50).

These people are heroes, but no more so than the retired businessman who volunteered a few days last year to work on a park event, the college student who spent a Saturday gathering names for a park-related petition, or the busy working mother who found an evening to help her local park group mail off its newsletter. You can act as a park advocate in any number of ways, and no matter how much time or energy you contribute, you'll find your efforts paying you back, whether with the chance to meet other park supporters in your community or with the satisfaction of knowing that you've given back some of what your park has given you.

Here are some basic ways to take action. Can you spare...?

A Few Hours a Month

•**Read and research:** Park-related issues and stories are at the forefront of the environmental movement. They are covered by most national and local newspapers, magazines, and television and radio stations. More information is available from public and private libraries, the Park Service and environmental organizations. Park advocates must first educate themselves on park issues before they can begin the process of educating others.

•**Get on your park's mailing list:** Parks maintain mailing lists of people who want to be informed of any management actions. Ask to be placed on the list for your park and stress that you want to be notified of any opportunities to participate in "scoping." (Scoping is an agency's solicitation of public opinion on an action.)

•**Join a local or national park advocacy organization:** Park groups rely on active membership bases to support programs, produce educational materials and increase the visibility of park issues among the media, elected officials, the Park Service and the general public. Most groups provide their members with newsletters. Local park advocacy groups have smaller memberships and fewer resources than their counterparts at the national level. Their members need to take a more active role in the day-to-day running of the organization. National park advocacy groups often recruit members to work on key park issues at the local level. (For a list of advocacy and friends groups associated with national parks, see Appendix C.)

•**Write a letter or make a phone call to an elected official:** Raise the level of awareness of your elected officials about park issues by writing or phoning them for their position. This will let them know that their constituents care about the problems facing national parks and are interested in how government works to solve these problems. An informed constituency creates a heightened response to park problems.

•**Write a letter to the editor of a local or national newspaper or magazine:** The news media can be a crucial help in raising the visibility of park issues and in stirring the support of local and national communities. (See Chapter 4, "Telling Your Story to the Media.")

One Day a Month

•**Attend the meeting of your local park group:** These meetings provide an opportunity to meet with other park advocates. It's also a good way to let others know you want to do something for your park.

•**Visit your park:** Become familiar with your park so that you are able to notice when the park is being improved, neglected or altered in any way. When you do notice a problem, be sure to alert park management. Either write to the superintendent and ask for a response, or call and ask for the person who handles the type of problem you are reporting. Also alert your local and national advocacy groups.

Become familiar with your park's staff and their duties. Most parks have a superintendent, assistant superintendent, chief of interpretation, natural and/or cultural resources manager and chief of maintenance, as well as field staff such as rangers. Set up a time to meet with the park staff. (Don't assume they don't have time for you. Remember: It's their job to serve the public.) It is helpful to know several members of the staff to get a full perspective on park needs. Check in with them regularly.

A Few Days a Month or More

•**Volunteer:** To do volunteer work, contact your park directly or contact the National Park Service Interpretation Division at (202) 619-7077 and ask for information on becoming a volunteer.

•**Participate in park planning:** National Park Service policies require public involvement. The general management plan is the comprehensive plan for your park and should guide day-to-day decisions made by park staff. Ask when the plan is scheduled to be revised and become familiar with the existing document so that you have a point of reference for any activity occurring in the park. Make sure you are on the park mailing list. Advocates should offer comments on all park management plans. (See Chapter 11 for more details on park planning.)

•**Build a network of people in your community interested in protecting your park:** If there is a park advocacy group in your area, become an active member and help recruit other interested park supporters. Seek to develop a well-rounded coalition that represents all aspects of the community. Include neighborhood leaders, local politicians, the chamber of commerce, members of local environmental groups and other park users. Reach out to people who might not think of themselves as park supporters or environmentalists. Most people think parks are important but don't recognize how parks affect their lives directly or that many parks are threatened.

Your involvement in protecting parks is more important now than ever before. As development pressures make open space increasingly scarce, ecosystems and wildlife habitat that depend on parks and their adjacent lands are being destroyed at an alarming rate. America's cultural heritage is being paved over to build suburban shopping malls. Park budgets are being cut at an even faster rate. The battle to protect our parks is on. A committed, vocal community of park advocates is key to winning the battle.

Chapter 2

Getting to Know the Park System

There is nothing so American as our parks. The scenery and wildlife are native. The fundamental idea behind the parks is native. It is, in brief, that the country belongs to the people...Parks stand as the outward symbol of this great human principle.

Franklin Delano Roosevelt

2

GETTING TO KNOW THE PARK SYSTEM

In the Beginning

Even though Arkansas' Hot Springs area and what would later be known as Yosemite National Park had been set aside for public enjoyment earlier, the creation of Yellowstone National Park in 1872 is usually credited as the beginning of the National Park System. In designating Yellowstone National Park, Congress established a new policy that portions of public lands were to be:

> ...reserved and withdrawn from settlement, occupancy or sale under the laws of the United States and dedicated and set apart as a public park or pleasuring ground for the benefit and enjoyment of the people.

Congress entrusted the preservation of "the natural curiosities and wonders" within Yellowstone to the Secretary of the Interior.

Initially, the areas set aside by Congress were scenic natural areas. However, in 1890, at the urging of veteran groups, the federal government consciously began preserving historic sites, starting with the establishment of Chickamauga and Chattanooga National Military Park in Tennessee and Georgia, the site of a famous Civil War conflict.

In 1906, Congress passed the Antiquities Act, which granted the President the authority to proclaim and reserve as national monuments "historic landmarks, historic and prehistoric structures, and other objects of historic or scientific interest." This was done largely to provide protection to prehistoric Indian ruins. President Theodore Roosevelt, however, used the monument authority to set aside significant natural areas as well, and later presidents followed suit for almost four decades.

In 1943, a controversy erupted that greatly reduced subsequent presidential use of the Antiquities Act. At the request of the Rockefeller family, President Franklin D. Roosevelt used the Antiquities Act to reserve 33,000 acres of land the family wished to donate as part of a larger Jackson Hole National Monument. Locals were outraged by the permanent protection of the land—it meant they'd lose hunting rights and tax revenues—and their protests moved congressional leaders to try to abolish the monument. Although their efforts failed and the land was eventually incorporated into Grand Teton National Park, presidential use of the Antiquities Act has been infrequent ever since. One exception occurred in 1978, when President Jimmy Carter designated 11 national monuments in Alaska to provide short-term protection until Congress could pass comprehensive park and wilderness legislation.

Geysers and other "natural curiosities" led Congress to designate Yellowstone the first national park in 1872.

New Agency for the New System

More than 40 years after the 1872 designation of Yellowstone, the National Park Service was established to manage the parks. During the late 1800s, the parks were under the direct authority of the Secretary of the Interior, but difficulties in protecting them from poaching and other abuses led Congress to authorize the Secretary to call upon the U.S. Army for help.

It was not until the loss of the spectacular Hetch Hetchy Valley in Yosemite National Park to a dam project in 1913 that park preservationists began a serious campaign to improve the management of the parks. One of the leading proponents, Chicago businessman Stephen T. Mather, was appointed assistant secretary for park matters. Within two years, Mather and an associate, Horace M. Albright, with the backing of a broad coalition of business and conservation interests, successfully lobbied Congress to create the National Park Service.

On August 26, 1916, President Woodrow Wilson signed the "Organic Act" that established the National Park Service. This act distinguished the Park Service from the other public land agencies of the time, whose missions were to exploit and extract resources. Instead, the Organic Act instructed NPS:

> to conserve the scenery and the natural and historic objects and the wild life therein and to **provide for the enjoyment** of the same in such manner and by such means as will leave them unimpaired for the enjoyment of future generations.

Additionally, the Organic Act gave the Secretary of the Interior the authority to make such rules and regulations as necessary for the use and administration of areas under the National Park Service. He could sell and dispose of timber under certain conditions and he could destroy animal and plant life that might be detrimental to the use of the park. He could grant leases for concessionaires and he could permit the grazing of livestock if it was deemed not detrimental to the area. (However, a special provision forbade grazing in Yellowstone.)

One of the earliest policy statements for the new Park Service was set down in a letter on May 13, 1918, from Secretary of the Interior Franklin K. Lane to Stephen Mather. In it Lane established that: the national parks must be maintained *unimpaired*; they are set apart for the *use and pleasure of the people*; and the *national interest must dictate all decisions* affecting public or private enterprise in the parks. He urged the encouragement of "educational, as well as recreational, use" of the parks, low-priced concessionaire-operated camps, a system of free campsites, no grazing, harmonizing of construction with the landscape, and expansion of the park system with areas of "supreme and distinctive quality."

Many of these policies remain in place today, although their interpretation has varied widely over the years. For example, during Mather's reign, "unimpaired" frequently meant "scenically pleasing" and had little to do with preserving natural processes. Forest fires and predators were considered blights upon the best views of parks, so a concerted campaign to eradicate both dominated the Park Service's early resource-management programs.

Stephen Mather feared that the newly created Park Service could become easily corrupted by political interests. In 1919, he encouraged a business associate, Robert Sterling Yard, to form a citizen watchdog group, the National Parks Association. Over the past decades, the Association has been instrumental in the protection and expansion of the National Park Service. It was renamed the National Parks and Conservation Association in 1970. (For more on NPCA, see Appendix B.)

Until the 1930s, the National Park Service consisted of a Washington bureau and staff at individual parks. The Civilian Conservation Corps (CCC), created by the federal government during the Depression, brought thousands of workers into more than 100 national parks. The CCC's regional structure evolved into a permanent regional structure for NPS. Today there are ten NPS regions. (See Appendix E for a list of the NPS regional offices and the states they include.)

More Popularity, More Problems

When the new Park Service was created, it took over the management of 14 national parks and 21 national monuments previously under the administration of the Department of Interior. All these areas had been carved out of the public domain. Then, in 1920, Congress set down a new policy which authorized the Secretary of Interior in his administration of the National Park Service to accept the donation of patented lands. Congress continued to add to the park system's numbers and began to include areas that perhaps were less scenically dramatic but which had unique ecosystems, such as Everglades National Park in Florida.

A major expansion of the National Park System occurred in 1933 when the Park Service was given responsibility for the more than 60 monuments and parks administered by other federal agencies. This event established for the first time a single federal system of parks and declared historic preservation as a major mission of the National Park Service.

Congress reaffirmed this mission in 1935 with the passage of the Historic Sites Act. The act served as the catalyst for the National Historic Landmark Program and gave the Secretary of the Interior the authority to survey and protect historic properties. It also created what is known today as the National Park System Advisory Board. Comprised of outside experts selected by the Secretary of Interior, the board advises the Secretary on potential new additions to the system and on park policy issues.

Furthermore, Congress also authorized interpretation programs for the first time—educational programs and services about the historically and naturally significant sites within American parklands.

War and Water Demands

In the 1940s, World War II demanded that America direct all its money, manpower and resources, natural and otherwise, to the war effort. This left the National Park Service operating with half its normal work force and budget. The parks became the site of military practice maneuvers and rehabilitation camps, and expansion of the Park System virtually ground to a halt. For years, developers had coveted the immense mineral and timber resources of the parks, but the demands for the war effort posed the most serious threat yet to the parks' resources.

In particular, the Sitka spruce forests of Olympic National Park were sought for the construction of aircraft.

Following the war, the untamed riverways of the parks, such as the Colorado in Grand Canyon, the Flathead in Glacier and the Green in Mammoth Cave, attracted dam proposals for hydropower development and flood control by the Bureau of Reclamation and the U.S. Army Corps of Engineers. Conservation organizations, including NPCA, led the opposition to these dam proposals. The only casualty of these battles was the Glen Canyon Dam, which impounds the Colorado above Grand Canyon National Park and has drastically altered the flow and sedimentation of the river through the Canyon.

Visitors, Visitors and More Visitors

Under the direction of Stephen Mather, the National Park Service promoted tourism to the parks as a way to foster public support. Many of the luxury hotels such as the El Tovar in the Grand Canyon and the Ahwanee in Yosemite were developed by the railroads to attract affluent Americans to travel by train to the parks.

The growing availability of the automobile, however, soon made even the most remote parks accessible to the American middle class. Parks were quickly inundated with visitors they were ill-equipped to serve. In 1922, barely one million people visited the parks. By 1950, that number had soared to 33 million. Today, nearly 300 million visitors flock to the parks annually. (See Chapter 8 for more on visitor impacts.)

In 1956, Congress launched the "Mission 66" program—a ten-year building and staffing program to upgrade and expand park services that was to culminate on the 50th anniversary of the National Park Service. The program resulted in the construction of dozens of visitor centers and other park-supported facilities. However, Mission 66's lasting value and impact on park environments are questioned by many who believed that it encouraged mass use of the parks at the expense of resource protection.

The 1960s and Beyond

The 1960s were a time of great expansion in both the way parklands were acquired and how they were managed. Up until this point, National Park System areas had largely been created out of public or donated lands. In 1961, Congress authorized Cape Cod National Seashore to be assembled mainly through the purchase or condemnation of private property. It also provided for the establishment of a park advisory commission comprising local and state interests. Many parks since have been established along the Cape Cod model.

The '60s also saw the creation of the Land and Water Conservation Fund (LWCF) to provide adequate outdoor recreation opportunities at the state and local levels. Money for the fund is derived from fees and royalties from offshore gas and oil drilling leases. LWCF has served as the chief source of money for land acquisition by federal land-managing agencies. Since 1965, approximately $4.7 billion has been appropriated for federal park, wildlife, wetland and recreation land acquisitions. (For more on LWCF, see Chapter 14, "Congress and the National Parks.")

Growing concern over the management of natural resources in the parks led to a report in 1963 by a panel of scientists headed by A. Starker Leopold, son of the famous conservationist Aldo Leopold. The panel stated:

As a primary goal, we would recommend that the biotic associations within each park be maintained, or where necessary recreated, as nearly as possible in the condition that prevailed when the area was first visited by the white man.

The report was the catalyst for a number of policy revisions for NPS, including the end of indiscriminate pesticide use, the reduction of fire-suppression programs, the elimination of non-native plants and animals, the restoration of wild predators, and the prohibition against feeding of bears and other wildlife.

American interest in preserving remaining wild areas resulted in the creation of the National Wilderness System (through the Wilderness Act of 1964) and the Wild and Scenic Rivers System (through the Wild and Scenic Rivers Act of 1968).

What's in a Designation?

Found in every state and territory in the U.S. except Delaware, the National Park System is more than a system of parks. It is a network of areas with a diversity unparalleled in the world.

Every area is not a "park" per se (although for simplicity's sake, we call them parks throughout this book); rather, there are more than 20 classifications or types of parks found in the Park System.

The best-known designation, **national park**, has been given to more than 50 areas. The vast majority of these are large natural areas, with only a few, such as Colorado's Mesa Verde National Park, the site of Anasazi cliff dwellings, having more of a cultural focus.

The most common designation, **national monument**, usually refers to areas that are smaller than national parks and that have less diverse nationally significant resources. The monument designation was largely reserved for areas that had a single prominent feature and was used to protect historic and prehistoric sites in the first part of this century. Now it is used for natural areas as well.

Today, more than 37 million acres of parklands have been designated as wilderness and more than 2,600 miles of rivers managed by the National Park Service have been designated as wild and scenic.

The National Historic Preservation Act of 1966 strengthened historic preservation authorities. The act authorized the federal government to accelerate its historic preservation programs and activities and established the Advisory Council on Historic Preservation.

Not all the parks laws passed in the '60s have adequately protected resource values. Passage of the Concessions Policy Act of 1965 instituted policies that have stifled competition, established low franchise fees and entrenched monopoly businesses in the parks. Administrative reform efforts have met with modest success in recent years, but a legislative overhaul of the program is currently being debated to ensure optimal visitor services in the parks while preserving park ecosystems.

The 1970s saw the passage of some of the most significant environmental laws on the books today, including the National Environmental Policy Act and the Clean Air Act (both in 1970), the Clean Water Act (in 1972) and the Endangered Species Act (in 1973). These bolstered legal protections for park resources. However, despite this new legislation, many park resources were found to be in poor condition and declining when the Park Service presented its *State of the Parks* report to Congress in 1980.

During the Reagan and Bush administrations in the 1980s, the condition of the National Park System only worsened. Under the administrative oversight of Reagan's Interior Secretary James Watt, the Park Service focused on facility enhancement rather than resource protection. One bright note in the '80s was Congress' spectacular near doubling of the Park System's total acreage, with the passage of the Alaska National Interest Lands Conservation Act in 1980 and the addition of more than 40 million acres of national parkland in Alaska.

Public Leadership Will Shape the Park System's Future

The National Park System was founded in an era of resource exploitation and abuse. The decade following the establishment of Yellowstone witnessed the virtual extermination of the millions of bison that once roamed the plains. In the intervening century, NPS has mirrored, and, in some cases, fostered the gradual enlightenment of the American public on environmental issues. Predators are no longer exterminated in the parks, and natural fires are, for the most part, allowed to burn. Instead of focusing on individual species, parks are employing an *ecosystem management* approach to resources.

Other classifications that have been applied to natural areas include **national lakeshores, national seashores, national rivers, wild and scenic riverways, national parkways,** and **national scenic trails**.

National preserves and **national reserves** are newer designations created by Congress in the early '70s. They provide for protection of natural resources, but also allow certain resource-consumptive activities specified by Congress, such as mineral extraction or hunting.

National recreation areas tend to be sizable natural areas that encompass man-made reservoirs or recreational resources located near urban centers.

A similar variety exists in the types of units that have a cultural focus. Two of the most common designations are **national historic site** and **national historical park**. The nation's military past also has been preserved in **national military parks, national battlefield parks, national battlefield sites**, and **national battlefields**. Structures or sites that commemorate an individual are often identified as **national memorials**.

Changes in attitudes and policies are also occurring in the management of cultural resources. Grave sites in archaeological ruins are no longer excavated, but respected as sacred burial grounds. Interpretation of historical events is broadening from a traditionally Eurocentric slant to encompass multicultural perspectives.

In 1991, on its 75th anniversary, the National Park Service assembled a team of park professionals, citizen advocates and resource experts to evaluate its programs and policies with an eye toward the next 25 years. The final report, *National Parks for the 21st Century* (better known as the "Vail Agenda"), outlined a specific agenda for the Park Service's action in four major areas: organizational renewal, park use and enjoyment, environmental leadership and resource stewardship.

It is still too early to see if this report will prove a catalyst for any significant change, but the challenges have been identified and targeted by both the public and the agency itself. Public support for the report's recommendations, however, will greatly increase the chances for their success. (For a copy of the "Vail Agenda," write to Ron Sarff, Mount Rainier National Park, Tahoma Woods, Star Route, Ashford, WA 98304-9801.)

Chapter 3

Forming a Park Advocacy Group

Our parks and preserves are not merely picknicking places. They are rich storehouses of memories and reveries. They are bearers of wonderful tales to him who will listen, a solace to the aged and an inspiration to the young.

Colonel Richard Lieber

3

FORMING A PARK ADVOCACY GROUP

Forming a park advocacy group takes dedication, but it can be easier than you imagine. Many parks (and parks-to-be) have advocacy organizations working to promote good environmental management. These groups work for the protection and preservation of their parks but are not funded or controlled by the National Park Service or state or local governments. Each is free to set its own priorities and budget. Find out what group or groups are working to protect the park near you already (see Appendix C for a list of advocacy groups). If there is no such group, or if they are not addressing park issues that concern you, consider forming your own. What follows is a series of suggested steps toward creating such a group.

Identify Core Support

Take the initiative to set up an introductory meeting with three or four individuals in your community who have demonstrated an interest in protecting the park. This group will serve as a catalyst in creating the core mission. Each of you needs to think through the mission of the organization to give the group direction. The initial mission may consist of broad statements that take many years to accomplish, but set your sights high. Efforts made early on will determine your group's course of action for years to come.

Set Up an Organizational Meeting

The next step is to formally create the advocacy group. To be effective, your citizens group must include a broad base of local park supporters, and these individuals must be invited to an organizational meeting. Clear goals, good publicity and a willingness to reach out to the local park constituency will help you find many people to help in your effort.

To identify these park supporters, you will want to hold a well-publicized organizational meeting. Set the meeting date well in advance so local and national environmental organizations can publicize the event. Identify local newspaper, radio and TV reporters who work on environmental stories. They may be able to give you some exposure. When working with the news media, remember that they need a story with broad interest. You need to do some homework and come up with interesting material for them. Use this opportunity to talk about issues that concern you in the management of the park. (For more tips on how to approach the media, see Chapter 4.)

At your organizational meeting, you may want to discuss:
- **the group's goals**
- **bylaws and nonprofit incorporation**
- **IRS tax status**
- **membership development and communication**
- **start-up funding**

Define Goals

Stick closely to your mission to support and protect the park. Straying from the core mission of an advocacy group can lead to ineffectiveness. Once this happens, the group becomes a marginal player at best. Be selective when choosing projects, and create annual and long-range agendas that are achievable. Break projects down to realistic goals, and make sure the right person is chosen to carry out a given duty.

Make it a goal to work cooperatively with park management while remaining independent. Although a citizens group works with park administrators, the group is not a tool for administrators' use. An advocacy group must maintain its autonomy. Members need to be clear about and comfortable with the group's advocacy role. Your group's goals will be incorporated into your by-laws, along with rules on election of offices, annual meetings, etc.

Incorporate as a Nonprofit Group

Contact the Secretary of State or other officials in your state to find out what you need to do to register as a nonprofit corporation. There may be requirements that you need to satisfy to qualify for nonprofit status. If an attorney is willing to volunteer to act as the group's agent, take advantage of that option. An agent doesn't necessarily have to be an attorney, however, and any well-organized individual with a permanent address can serve as one. To qualify for federal tax-exempt status, you will want to include a statement on the group's educational and scientific purposes and the disposition of assets to other nonprofit organizations if your group should dissolve.

Obtain Nonprofit Tax Status

You will want to get a copy of the federal IRS publication on nonprofit tax status before you file the articles of incorporation with the state. If you want contributors to be able to take deductions on their income tax, you will need to file for the appropriate status, probably chapter 501(c)3. If you are granted 501(c)3 status, you are limited in the amount of funds that can be expended on federal lobbying efforts.

If the area that is the focus of your interest is not currently a part of the National Park System, and if you plan on funding several trips to Washington, D.C., to testify in support of legislation and lobby members of Congress, then you may wish to consider other alternatives. One option would be to establish a chapter 501(c)3 foundation as an auxiliary organization and use the "tax-free" donations only for nonpolitical purposes. Here again, working with an attorney may be helpful, but any person willing to take the time to carefully read the rules and instructions can figure it out. IRS tax status decisions are slow, and the first decision is provisional and could be changed by a higher authority. However, contributors can rely on your application when making a contribution, as the decision is retroactive.

Some foundations and corporate donors will not consider

Profile: Louis Skrmetta

Louis Skrmetta and his son, Peter III, age 5

From the pristine white sand beaches of Hope Island, you can see the emerald gulf water and barrier islands along the coast of Mississippi. Today that view is unobstructed, thanks largely to the efforts of Louis Skrmetta and his organization, the Gulf Islands Conservancy.

For three generations, the Skrmetta family has planted new roots here, after immigrating west from the Croatian island of Brac, off the Dalmation coast. Since Louis' grandfather, Pete, began skippering oyster schooners and shrimp boats here in 1905, new families of Skrmettas have set down roots in the South, helping run a summer tour operation that ferries Mississippians to the balmy beach repose of the barrier islands.

Since 1971, the islands have been protected as the Gulf Islands National Seashore. But that didn't shelter them from the regional threats outside of park boundaries which eventually gave rise to the conservancy, and which ultimately led 38-year-old Louis, the eldest of four Skrmetta brothers who used to lead backpacking trips and guide boats to the islands, to learn the ropes of environmental activism while he helped run the family business.

Unlike the Texas and Louisiana coastlines, the Mississippi gulf coast has escaped the oil boom. But even after the barrier islands were designated as a national seashore, they did not escape a new industrial threat. It arrived in 1990 in the form of a proposal to anchor a series of 550-foot barges—floating fish farms—which, through the depositing of medicated fish feed, threatened to create a marine "dead zone" just a mile offshore. The fish farms would be anchored a quarter-mile outside of park boundaries, and National Park Service officials were powerless to prevent it.

"We'd been dodging the bullet all these years," Skrmetta says. "The oil companies have been offshore in Louisiana; environmental threats had always been their problem. This was the first bona fide threat to the seashore."

The Skrmettas consulted with the National Park Service. "I sat across from my father and we said, 'Can't you do anything about it?' They said no. The Park Service isn't a regulatory agency. They didn't have the authority." Louis, who had skipped law school to help run the business, and who had earned a living piloting the same boats as his grandfather Pete, suddenly began poring over environmental studies, writing position papers and building coalitions.

"These islands are like my own property," Skrmetta explains. "I don't own them, but I was raised out there on the boats with my dad and grandfather. I knew how beautiful they were, foresaw the beginning of everything that makes them special—the sandy beaches, the saltwater marshes—so when these barges came, we didn't have much choice but to do something. Those islands are our livelihood. And if fish farms had been allowed to anchor offshore, what would be next? Garbage barges from New York?"

Louis began calling people across the country to collect information, and poring over scientific data to collect the evidence needed to make an argument to state legislators. Meanwhile, the conservancy's 50 or so volunteers—half of them from other parts of the country who'd visited the Gulf Coast and "adopted" it—sent off letters to state legislators, warning them of the environmental consequences of the fish farming. The Sierra Club Legal Defense Fund joined the

battle, offering to represent the conservancy against the state. Skrmetta wrote op-ed pieces for local papers, put together fact sheets for local politicians, the Chamber of Commerce and other pro-tourism groups, attended public hearings and spoke to groups who'd listen, like the Lion's Club.

"We were just little people," says Skrmetta. "We weren't up in Jackson wining and dining the Department of Agriculture or anything—but we were able to come in at the last minute and get the word out." After a year and a half of consistent pressure from the conservancy, the state made more stringent its guidelines for marine aquaculture and, finally, the industry lease for the fish farm was withdrawn. Diplomacy, Skrmetta discovered, goes a lot farther in the South than a "radical approach" to environmental protection. As Skrmetta puts it, "The people didn't say 'Hell, no'—just no."

While Skrmetta splits his time between environmental advocacy and eco-tourism—battling Gulf Coast casino development is his latest challenge—his own sons, Robert, 7, and five-year-old Peter Skrmetta III, are now riding the boats on the 12-mile trip out to Hope Island during summer vacations. They're tour boats, not shrimp schooners, but the legacy seems genuine.

grant requests from organizations that do not have their federal tax status confirmed. For this reason, you may want to start on the paperwork early. Having nonprofit status with the IRS also makes it easier and faster to get a nonprofit franking permit from the post office. (See below.)

Develop Your Group's Membership

Organizational members range from the active to the inactive. Some members are content just to write checks to fund the organization or to fund a specific campaign. More active members may want to involve themselves in the day-to-day activities of the organization or be contacted as needed for campaign mailings and other organizational projects. Some members have business or political contacts while others have connections with local environmental activists. That's why it's important to keep track of member participation and involve them according to their diverse strengths.

It's important to communicate with your members on a regular basis. Depending on the organization's resources, a timely newsletter should be sent to each member alerting them to the group's accomplishments, park events, park legislation, member activities and meeting times. A newsletter brings a certain professionalism to the organization and will keep members and other area and national organizations abreast of key park issues. An informed membership is an active membership.

Start a Mailing List

From the beginning, you will want to work on a mailing list. If one of your group's potential members has a computer with a mailing list program, your task will be much easier.

Your mailing list can and should include more than the paid membership. Your congressional delegation, Park Service personnel at the park and regional office, activists in other environmental organizations, media and other potential allies should be included. Even a small organization can develop a stable mailing list of more than 200 names.

•Post Office Nonprofit Franking Permit

Communicating by mail with your membership and friends

will be the primary way to keep interest high and to achieve your goals. If each mailing consists of at least 200 pieces and you mail at least once a year, a nonprofit franking permit will help reduce your mailing costs. If you want to maintain an accurate mailing list, you need to mail at least every six months, as that is how long the post office retains forwarding addresses. An initial fee is required with your application. Only certain post offices accept bulk mail, and you must always mail at the same post office. For this reason, you will want to pick a location that is convenient to several potential mailing coordinators. In each mailing, all of the pieces must be identical in weight and content.

Apply for Start-Up Funding

Starting an organization requires a great deal of time, and you will have expenses that are more than a small group can dedicate out of pocket. Help is available. Your public library has books and reference manuals on how to apply for grants. These include a book of foundations with notes on the types and sizes of grants they are most likely to consider. Look for start-up funding from retailers in your area. Service retailers located near a park have a financial stake in the well-being of the park. Encourage them to support you or at least join you in your efforts.

Outdoor retailers, even if they are not located near your park, have become big supporters of grassroots environmental protection efforts. For instance, Recreation Equipment Incorporated (REI), a user-owned cooperative selling outdoor equipment, makes grants of $1,000 and allows one-time access to their mailing list for start-up costs and publicity of new environmental groups. Their address is 1525 11th Avenue, Seattle, WA 98122. North Face, LL Bean, Patagonia, and others may also consider an application. Your best bet is to look for retailers that have a particular interest in your park. For example, if your group is forming to protect a Wild and Scenic River, you might seek out a kayak company or rafting operation. Generally, it is easier to get start-up funds than operating funds. You should plan to finance your annual operating expenses from dues, and use grant funds for special projects and start-up costs. Foundations may require proof of nonprofit status before making a grant.

It takes commitment and determination to succeed in building a base from which a viable citizens group can grow. But with some effort you can develop a cadre of dedicated park advocates. You may be amazed by what your group can accomplish with a little organization and perseverance. Just when your arms tire from folding mailers or your voice falters on the phone tree, new members and volunteers will join your group and bolster membership. They will want to give something back for their experience in the park, and if you offer a visible, attractive path, they will join you.

Chapter 4

Telling Your Story to the News Media

Nature cannot be ordered about, except by obeying her.

Francis Bacon

Note: Material in this chapter was adapted with permission from the *Superintendent's Guide to Public Affairs*, a 1988 National Park Service handbook by Duncan Morrow and William G. Thomas.

TELLING YOUR STORY TO THE NEWS MEDIA

Getting the word out on issues concerning your park requires the help of the news media. Dealing with the media, whether it is reporters and editors in print (newspapers and magazines), radio or television, does not need to be difficult. By following a few simple guidelines, you can relate critical information effectively. The most important thing to remember is that you must have *real* news to offer if you issue a press release or hold a news conference. If you have no news the first time, you'll have no news coverage the next time.

Preparing News Releases

To get your message across to the news media, you must present the facts. The vehicle for doing this is a written news release. News releases are used to document policy statements and events such as public meetings.

•What Editors Want

If you do not want your news release to end up in an editor's wastebasket, it must be:

- Newsworthy—No news is bad news!
- Appropriate—Tailor it to for the audience of the publication/station to which you are sending it.
- "Punchy"—If your "lead" doesn't grab an editor at the start, they won't be around for the finish.
- Well-written—This is especially important for smaller

publications, which have less time and staff available to edit and/or rewrite.

- Illustrated—Charts, graphs and especially photographs will help you "sell" your story.

•Elements of the News Release

Every news release you prepare should include the following elements:

- Contact person—The person named should be readily available to answer questions concerning the subject of the release. Always include both first and last names and phone numbers.
- Date of release—In most cases, use "For Immediate Release," followed by the date you are issuing your release. If you are releasing information that will be publicly presented on a future date, you might use a future release date such as "For Release Thursday, June 27."
- Headline—At the top of your story, put a headline in capitals. It should be underlined. Just as you look at headlines to decide if you want to read a story in the newspaper, an editor looks at the hundreds of news releases received every day to decide which he or she will cover. Write terse headlines that say something. For example:

NATIONAL PARKS GRAVELY ENDANGERED, REPORT FINDS

is far better than

PARKS GROUP ISSUES NEW REPORT

Other guidelines to remember include:

- Keep it short and to the point.
- Double space all text to leave room for editing. Provide generous margins. Try to keep your release to one page. If it is longer than a single page, use only one side of the paper. (Newspaper, radio and television editors prefer this. Remember, you are not saving paper if the editor throws your release in the wastebasket!)

• Indent at the beginning of each paragraph—the way stories appear in the newspaper.

•Writing Your News Release

When writing your news release, use simple sentences that give all the important facts. A reporter will call you with any questions about details or for background on the facts you provide.

Your first paragraph should summarize what the release is about. Your goal is to answer all the important questions in just a few lines of copy. This way, if an editor only has room for a brief item, he or she can tell the whole story in one paragraph. If an editor has to hunt through your release for the facts, chances are he or she won't bother.

After the lead paragraph, write the rest of your news release in logical order. Use simple sentences and short paragraphs. Be sure your release answers all the basic journalistic questions of Who, What, When, Where, Why and How.

•Photographs and Captions

Illustrations, especially photographs, are in high demand. For print media, they add visual interest to the news item. For television, they indicate what the camera crew will find if they come to cover your event.

Try to avoid pictures of people shaking hands (known to editors as "grip-and-grin" shots). Give them something better if you can. And remember, newspapers prefer 8" x 10" glossy prints for black and white, and 35mm slides for color. Television uses black-and-white pictures when no color is available; color slides are sometimes useful to provide a backdrop for an on-camera reporter.

Always include a caption for pictures you provide. Captions should be complete, telling who and what are in the picture (with people's names spelled correctly and their location in a group shot identified). If the picture illustrates an event, be sure the caption notes when and where the event will occur. Be sure you have the photographer's permission to use the pictures you provide to the media, and always include a photo credit (such as "Photo by James Smith") in your caption.

Cultivating the Media

Every news organization has a person who screens incoming information, determines which items have news potential, and directs how the news organization will respond. This person may be an assignment editor, city editor, feature editor, news editor or, in the cases of radio and television, news director. Whatever this person's title, this is someone you need to know. Make an appointment for a brief professional meeting. Introduce yourself, state your business, then respect their busy schedule and leave.

After you've made this initial contact, reach these people with simple messages. Send them an "Editors Advisory" announcing the event you would like them to cover. This will help get a reporter assigned to your event.

The advisory is particularly valuable in soliciting television coverage. Include a brief description of what will happen, and don't forget the visual aspects—note what there will be to photograph.

EDITORS ADVISORY

Contact: Sue Public 234-5678
Event: Annual March for Parks

More than 1,000 local citizens walking to raise money for Your Local Park. This year, 30 handicapped teenagers will participate in wheelchairs.

Time: 11:00 a.m., Sunday, April 20
Place: Your Park, Your Street,
        Your Town
Who: Governor Joe Smith and
        Mayor Jane Jones to speak

•Distributing News Releases

News organizations want to capture the interest of their audiences. If your release will help them do that, they will use it. If not, don't send it. Use releases only when you have something worth taking an editor's time. An editor who receives too many releases with too little news value from an individual or organization soon learns to ignore everything that comes from that source.

•Creating a Mailing List

To create a local mailing list, find out what newspapers are sold around town or around your park. Make sure you include the weeklies. Start your list with these. If free advertising tabloids are sent in the mail or left at checkout counters in local stores, add those that include news material. Find out what radio and television stations carry local news. Check with your local cable TV company: It probably has a local-access news or information program.

To create a regional mailing list, get the names of the nearest wire service bureaus, the news outlets that serve a major portion of your park's out-of-town visitors and regional magazines, many of which are marketed to serve a city, state or sub-state region. If you do not know the name of a specific reporter at the media organizations on your list, address your releases as follows:

Daily newspapers:	City Editor
Weekly newspapers:	Editor
Magazines:	Editor
Radio stations:	News Department
TV stations:	News Director

Send news releases to specific individual reporters who have helped you in the past. Cultivate those relationships. But remember to keep track of your media contacts and keep your list up-to-date as reporters move or are reassigned frequently.

Don't try to save postage by putting more than one release in the same envelope. Since different stories are likely to be assigned to different reporters, this may cause one of your releases to be ignored or lost. Always package photographs in a rigid mailer or with cardboard.

Know the deadlines of the news media you deal with. Most feature departments (such as travel sections) and magazines have deadlines long before things appear in print—often six weeks or more. Weekly papers need releases just before their weekly deadlines. The daily media are best equipped to act on a release received on a weekday. Time your mailings accordingly.

•Additional Background Materials

You may also want to produce materials that can provide invaluable general background on your group and on important issues. These can help you provide additional background for your news releases. Such materials may include:

- •Fact sheets—a collection of basic background information, listed in "bullet" form, on your event or issue.
- •Photographs—generic pictures—both 35mm slides and black-and-white glossy prints—that can help illustrate the issues and events in which you are involved (such as scenic shots or pictures of park users/volunteers).

Public Service Announcements

Radio and television stations generally broadcast a certain number of Public Service Announcements ("PSAs") for nonprofit community groups. This is a good way to get publicity, particularly for a community event such as a March for Parks.

Most stations like something that takes their announcer 30 seconds or less to read. Write your PSA as if you were going to speak it. Most people speak an average of 160 words per minute, or 80 words in 30 seconds. PSAs are written to be 60, 30, 20, 15 or 10 seconds—never more than 60 seconds.

Five weeks in advance of when you would like it broadcast, mail your PSA to the Public Service Director of each radio and television station in your area.

Public Service Announcements must be clearly marked with start and stop dates. This lets the Public Service Director know when the announcement is timely—and avoids the embarrassment of having the station announce an event that has already taken place.

Notice that in Public Service Announcement scripts, sentences are short. Numbers should be kept to a minimum because listeners often have trouble absorbing them. If numbers must be included, key numbers are often repeated in the text. Remember when timing your script that numbers will be read aloud as separate words.

PUBLIC SERVICE ANNOUNCEMENT

Contact: Richard James (202)123-4567
START DATE: 10/16/91
END DATE: 11/1/91

The National Parks and Conservation Association needs your help. Be a coordinator for our annual March for Parks. Involve your group in a local March. Be a March volunteer.

The March for Parks will take place May 1 through 3, 1994. To find out how you can be involved, call NPCA, toll-free, at 1-800-NAT-PARK.

That's 1 - 800 - N - A - T - P - A - R - K.

Interviews

If you are successful in generating interest from the news media on a project or issue, chances are good that you will be asked for an interview by one or more reporters. Always be prepared to answer reporters' questions. Your media interview will go smoothly if you follow these basic guidelines every time you talk with a reporter.

- Know your subject—Reporters are rarely specialists. Good ones will try to do some research before an interview, but in general it is your job to make certain the reporter understands what you are talking about.
- Always speak for the record—The surest way to avoid being quoted about something you don't want on the

public record is to avoid saying it.

- Always tell the truth—Only cite facts and statistics you can back up. Don't exaggerate. If you are caught in a lie, news reporters have two stories: Their first story is the truth and their second is your effort to conceal the truth. If you don't know the answer to a question, say so. Even experts need to refresh their memories.
- Respect deadlines—Every reporter has a deadline. If a broadcast reporter must file a story at 4 p.m. to get it on the evening news, don't delay the interview until 3:30. Even magazines have deadlines. Just because a story won't be published for six weeks, don't assume the reporter has six weeks to write it. Many magazines stop taking material weeks before the publication date. The rest of the time is taken up by editing, design, layout and printing—all processes beyond the reporter's control.
- Remember that reporters are not your enemies— Rarely will reporters try to trick or trap you. They want to get the story right, because failing to do so makes them look bad. Most "misquotations" are the result of failings on the part of the person being interviewed. It is not a misquotation if you regretted saying something once you saw it in print. It is no misrepresentation if you failed to explain your point clearly, leaving the reporter to make an erroneous interpretation of what you meant. Don't let a reporter choose your words for you. If the reporter says something like, "Then what you mean is," pay attention. You are about to hear how you will be quoted, unless you correct any mistake in the statement that follows.
- Never say "No comment" to a reporter on deadline—If you do not wish to answer a question, you can say, "I cannot give out that information because..." and tell them why. Or you can say, "I don't know. I'll check and call you back." This is a great response. It means you are willing to be helpful.

When dealing with reporters from a specific medium, you should bear in mind the following suggestions:

- Print Media—Learn what the publication's readership is. Prepare accordingly. Newspapers and magazines have a great capacity for reporting details. Know the ones that are relevant. Think about the key statements you might make. Use notes if you need to.
- Radio—Numbers sound terrible on radio. So do rambling answers. Be succinct. Be brief. Be to the point. If you have to think through an answer, do it before you start. An editor can eliminate a pause before the answer much more easily than one in the middle of your statement.
- Television—Just before a TV interview, visit a mirror. Check to see your hair is combed, there's no food between your teeth, etc. Otherwise, the rules are much like those for radio. Be prepared for the camera operator to ask you to repeat an answer just to get a different camera angle. They also may ask for casual footage of you talking with the reporter. Focus on something, either the interviewer or a point just past the camera. Most of us can't focus on the camera long enough to avoid looking shifty when the footage is shown on television. An unfocused gaze or wandering eyes are quite noticeable to a television viewer. Don't fidget. Be yourself.

Staging a Public Event

Chances are that at some point you will need to help organize and stage some sort of public event—a groundbreaking, March for Parks, dedication or other ceremony to which the public and VIPs are invited. To do this successfully, planning is essential. A checklist and timetable for all of the innumerable details should be devised, and revised as plans unfold. In planning your event, follow these basic guidelines:

- Think of a theme—Even the smallest ceremony takes place for a reason. Emphasize this theme in the invitation, printed program and publicity so that as many

Profile: Dan Trevisani

"I'm not someone who likes being in the camera or print," explains Dan Trevisani on a graveyard break at the firehouse in Utica. "I just like to do the work." The work he mentions—outside of fighting fires—is a public effort he coordinated two years ago to rehabilitate a large tract of parkland in the town of Utica, a working-class suburb east of Syracuse, New York. Proctor Park, a swathe of gentle, forested hills, cut by winding creeks and ponds, foot trails and stone bridges, has been the city's primary recreation and park area since it was handed over to the city in 1939 by wealthy tenants. Trevisani—along with eight brothers and two sisters—spent a good deal of his childhood in the park, going on family picnics, playing softball and frisbee.

But little by little in recent years, as park maintenance funds were cut from the city budget, Proctor sunk into disrepair. Litter piled up in picnic areas, grass and brush grew to waist high, bridges and roads fell apart. "You couldn't even walk through it," Trevisani recalls. "The money went downhill, and one by one, the whole place fell apart. The city just let it go."

Thirty-year-old Trevisani still lives nearby the park he played in as a child. He'd watched the park—and several old stately mansions within its borders, once the heart of the old city—idly deteriorating for years. The gregarious Trevisani decided enough was enough.

"Maybe I couldn't save the mansions, because they're private," he says. "But the park was *our* land, public land. And I decided we were

50

going to save it."

With the help of a pickup truck, a few buddies, and the local media, Trevisani "saved" Proctor Park in exactly two hours. The makeshift work crew carted away 10 truckloads of brush, trash and debris, and the local papers took notice. Says Trevisani, "I thought if we could do that in two hours, we could do the whole park in two weeks. I told a reporter about it, and the whole thing just took off."

But without the media's help, he admits, it couldn't have happened. "I knew I couldn't keep volunteers forever. I said to this reporter, 'I just need a little help. These folks just need a little pat on the back. That's all they want, a little mention in the local paper, something.'"

Work crews began to clean up two decades worth of park neglect in only a few weeks. But the question remained: how would the park be maintained in the future? Park maintenance demanded funding, and Trevisani once again looked to the media. "Here's my theory," he says. "Without media, there's no awareness. Without awareness, there's no participation."

Trevisani and about five other volunteers founded a Utica Parks Foundation and soon launched a public fundraising campaign, a March for Parks drive sponsored by NPCA. Trevisani, who was accustomed to spending late nights at the firehouse, found himself in meetings at newspapers and local radio and television stations, soliciting sponsorship donations. "I basically said if you don't sponsor us, the next guy will. That's how I sold

it to them. I had two radio stations fighting over who could become the main sponsor."

In six weeks, the foundation received three media sponsorships worth $6,000 apiece, and $6,000 in cash donations. T-shirts, hats, banners—and dozens of local newspaper stories which followed—advertised the effort. Finally, on a cold Sunday morning in Utica, 300 locals marched for Proctor Park.

Never before had this working class town rallied around an environmental cause, but Trevisani and his door-to-door volunteers worked hard at stirring up civic pride. "People didn't want to be known as being from the town with the dirty park. That really got 'em going."

State officials noticed, too. Not long after the March for Parks, they committed $50,000 to repair the park's deteriorating restrooms. The foundation also implemented its first user-permit system, and bottles have even been banned. A one-inch-thick stack of xeroxed articles about the Save the Park efforts attests to Trevisani's handiwork with the media.

"When you get people together, the media likes that. You have to coordinate a fantastic show—show 'em, 'Hey, look what we can do.' Once you show the media that the public cares, they respond."

Trevisani is now busy preparing for another March for Parks, and admits the job's become a little easier. "There were folks before who'd skeptically write a check for $10. Now they say, 'Oh yeah, I remember—you're the parks guy. Let's go.'"

elements as possible can be used to reinforce it.

- Select a date and place—In choosing a date for your event, make sure your event does not conflict with other programs that might attract the same audience or media.
- Devise a "rain" plan—Even indoor events can be affected by weather. Think about contingency plans before you need them. This way, they can be announced to the public and the media in time for your event to run smoothly.

•Media Arrangements

For media events, issue radio public service announcements to be used until the day of the event with the message that "this event is open to the public." Issue a general news release 10 to 14 days ahead of the event. This will alert the media and the public that an event is scheduled. Issue an Editors Advisory 7 to 10 days before the event to local print and electronic media. The advisory gives a brief description of the elements of your event that merit media attention.

Prepare a press kit for the media. Include background news releases, a list of platform guests, the printed program, and background information on the reason for the event. If available, add copies of key speeches and photographs of the principal speakers.

•Speakers

Speakers and other VIPs deserve a special invitation. Letters should include not only the time, place and date of the event, but the role you want the invitee to play, a description of the event, anticipated audience size, other anticipated speakers, media coverage, and a description of related events, such as luncheons, tours or receptions. When inviting speakers, remember that *very rarely* should a program run more than 60 minutes.

Speakers should be chosen for their relationship to the project, their position and their interest in the event. Make sure you have firm commitments from the speakers, then follow up with them to provide additional information on the length of their speech, their topic, details on transportation arrangements, accommodations and any other special needs they may have. Don't forget to find out if they will be accompanied by spouses, children or others who may need special seating.

Prepare a detailed, timed script of the program and give a copy to the master of ceremonies and each speaker. Always set aside a special "holding room" for speakers, and make sure they know that it is available before they arrive for the program. This allows speakers a place to relax before they appear on stage, and gives the event coordinator a sure way of knowing that speakers have arrived and if last-minute program changes are needed.

•Physical Arrangements

If you are using a platform, remember that each platform guest must be introduced. This takes time. A good general rule is to confine platform seating to no more than 20 people. Use a prepared seating chart for platform guests.

Be sure lighting is adequate. If the event is outside, consider where the sun will be—both for platform speakers and photographers. Check your sound system.

Plan for a special media section for photographers, reporters, television cameras and radio. Be sure you talk in advance with television and radio crews about arrangements for special hookups, outlets, lighting, and placement of the press section. Do not assign seating in the press area.

For any large event, make certain that trained personnel are available to provide on-site first-aid treatment. Keep a route clear for emergency vehicles. News media and VIP areas should be roped off.

•Follow-up

Make arrangements to obtain news clippings. Forward copies to your principal speakers. Always follow up with thank-you letters to participants, speakers and volunteers. Once the event is over, evaluate your efforts: What went right? What went wrong? Write up a simple report, making note of unexpected items and including suggestions for improvements. Your experience may help you or others do even better with a future event.

Conducting a Successful
Public Relations Campaign

If you are involved in an ongoing effort, like rallying community opposition to a development project that poses a potential threat to your park, you will have to work within the framework of a broader public relations strategy. There are four tactics basic to any effective public relations campaign:

- Create an emotional appeal—Know what is at stake in a given conflict. If it is the scenic beauty, the historic legacy or the health of the ecosystem within your park, an appeal to people's emotional ties to the park can prompt concern and action.

- Frame the issue—Don't let the opposition frame the debate by diverting attention away from the larger issue (the danger facing your park) to complex details that can dilute the force of your argument. It is your job to frame the issue clearly, in a way people will understand. If you lose the "black-and-white" focus of your cause, you will likely lose people's attention.

- Simplify grassroots action—Once you have people's attention, make it easy for them to help your cause. If you have a basic fact sheet, on the back you might list specific names and addresses people can contact to voice their opposition to the potential threat, either government officials or news media. Encourage public involvement by hosting events where people can learn more about the issue and at which you provide opportunities for their direct, immediate involvement, either by providing petitions or by having pens, paper and pre-stamped envelopes handy for letter writing.

- Identify an effective spokesperson—An effective spokesperson is knowledgeable, confident and persuasive. It is important that he or she be able to command attention and, when necessary, make an impassioned case for your park. While a nationally-known spokesperson can generate much needed attention, a local leader who has a thorough knowledge of the issue at hand can be just as effective, if not more so.

Chapter 5

Protecting Parks from External Threats

It is the main duty of government, if not the sole duty of government, to provide means of protection for all its citizens in the pursuit of happiness against the obstacles, otherwise insurmountable, which the selfishness of individuals or combinations of individuals is liable to interpose to that pursuit...Contemplation of natural scenes not only gives pleasure for the time being, but increases the subsequent capacity for happiness and the means of securing happiness.

Frederick Law Olmsted

5

PROTECTING PARKS FROM EXTERNAL THREATS

As you approach Zion National Park from the south, you see an arc of steep red sandstone cliffs, a spectacular view which may be obscured by a giant movie theater, a 200-space parking lot and 12,000 square feet of retail shopping—coming soon to the edge of the park, if World Odyssey Incorporated has its way. (Ironically, the proposed IMAX theater will show a film about Zion.)

Developers hope to drill the 1.3 million acres of North Dakota badlands surrounding Theodore Roosevelt National Park for oil and natural gas, leaving the rolling prairie dotted with derricks. The U.S. Forest Service has approved the plan to lease them the land and there are already 20 working sites within two miles of the park borders.

Similarly, in the not-too-distant future, visitors to Joshua Tree National Monument may wonder at the presence of scavenging ravens and the constant low rumbling of dumptrucks. The explanation could be Eagle Mountain Landfill, the world's largest proposed solid waste dump, which the Bureau of Land Management and Riverside County, California may allow to be constructed a mere 8,000 feet from the monument's border.

Parks were once seen as isolated enclaves preserved within impermeable boundaries. After a century of population growth and economic development, however, it has become clear that the integrity of parks' natural and cultural resources is dependent on interactions with the large and complex systems that surround them.

External threats are wide ranging, from urban sprawl to oil, gas and geothermal development. What impact will these threats have on the delicate ecosystems within park borders? How will they affect our experience and enjoyment of our national parks? Most importantly, how can we protect our parks from the forces at work beyond their boundaries?

While government is often passive about addressing external threats to the parks, you can play a crucial role in identifying and helping to avert external threats. Park advocates can ensure that public and private institutions are responsive to external threats and force compliance with the statutory and regulatory codes on which park protection rests. Citizen action can be the first, and last, line of defense—the difference between an intact park legacy and irreparable damage caused by activities outside the parks.

The External Threat Problem

In its 1980 *State of the Parks* report to Congress, the National Park Service identified strip mining, clear cutting, air pollution, a nuclear waste dump and other commercial, industrial, agricultural and residential development activities adjacent to parks as potential threats to national parks. All told, the report catalogued more than 4,000 harmful activities occurring in the lands surrounding parks.

Subsequent reports have concluded that these threats are getting worse. Surprisingly, the origins of one-third to one-half of these threats have been traced to the actions of other federal agencies and government organizations. Federal agencies such as the Bureau of Land Management and the U.S. Forest Service often manage the land adjacent to national parks. Unlike the Park Service, they are mandated to provide for the "multiple use" of their lands—including such uses as logging, mineral and geothermal development, and oil and gas exploration. Nationwide, the U.S. Forest Service oversees 190 million acres, the BLM 270 million.

The consequences of external threats to parks can be severe.

Development can: pollute air and water quality; lower water tables and drain groundwater; impede or destroy wildlife migration routes and habitat; cause the spread of nonnative plants and animals into the parks; disrupt park visibility and scenic views; and detract from visitors' enjoyment of the parks in general. The changes that development brings often create a need for more intensive management to protect the features that make the parks special.

Newton Drury, a former director of the National Park Service, once said: "If we are going to succeed in preserving the greatness of the national parks, they must be held inviolate. They represent the last stand of primitive America. If we are going to whittle away at them, we should recognize, at the very beginning, that such whittlings are cumulative and the end result will be mediocrity. The greatness will be gone."

Today, the evidence of such "whittlings" is everywhere. From proposals for a shopping mall next to Gettysburg

As urban populations continue to expand, suburban sprawl, such as these tracts of housing on the outskirts of Las Vegas, draw a fatal noose around pristine parklands.

National Military Park, to air pollution shrouding Shenandoah National Park, clear-cutting next to Olympic National Park, and drilling for oil, gas, and geothermal energy next to Yellowstone National Park, a fatal noose of development is being drawn tighter and tighter around the National Park System.

Legal Underpinnings of Park Protection

Park advocates should have a basic understanding of how environmental and park-related laws are made, interpreted and challenged. The web of laws and regulations will probably seem daunting at first, but comprehending it is essential to developing effective strategies for fighting park threats.

A complicated network of federal laws binds the National Park Service and the Secretary of the Interior to the duty of protecting parks, while other laws and regulations impose duties on other federal agencies. The basic legal underpinnings of park protection and management are drawn from the Organic Act (see page 21). Although the Organic Act recognized a dynamic tension between "preservation and use," conservationists have always interpreted the law to put primary emphasis on the former. "Unimpairment" is the standard by which our parks are to be managed and protected.

In terms of "external threats" and adjacent land use, the fundamental legal question, which has been the subject of a long-running debate, is the specific reach of the Organic Act outside of park boundaries. There are really two questions here: 1) What duty and authority does the Secretary of the Interior have to control activities outside parks, or on private land, that may be adversely affecting parks? 2) Does protecting parks have "primacy" in law, and in the decision-making process of federal agencies, over all other considerations?

The issues have been interpreted by the courts for years. While a large body of legal precedent has built up that strongly influences government actions and has a bearing on how successful park advocates are in challenging external threats, currently there is no universal, perfect legal weapon to which either NPS or park advocates can turn for ironclad protection.

Still, you should not be intimidated by legal limitations. Despite the uncertainties, you should be familiar with some particularly important park protection legal precedents. In 1978, as a result of a series of lawsuits by conservationists trying to halt damage to California's Redwood National Park from logging on adjacent lands, Congress clarified that the Secretary of the Interior's responsibilities under the Organic Act included protecting the national parks from harmful external activities. Congress amended the Organic Act to state that:

The protection, management, and administration of [national parks] shall be conducted in light of the high public value and integrity of the National Park System and shall not be exercised in derogation of the values and purposes for which these various areas have been established, except where specifically authorized by Congress.

Thus, a "nonimpairment" or "nonderogation" standard was reinforced for the parks. It is the legitimate standard that you should quote, and by which you should defend the parks when adjacent-lands issues arise, especially issues involving another federal agency within the Department of the Interior.

Many other federal laws are also important for park protection. Laws such as the Federal Land Policy and Management Act (governing administration of Bureau of Land Management lands), the National Forest Management Act (governing U.S. Forest Service activities), the Wild and Scenic Rivers Act, the Clean Water Act, the Clean Air Act, and the National Environmental Policy Act (NEPA) contain important park-related provisions. NEPA has had a particularly widespread effect on the activities of the federal government, and many federal agencies have policy statements regarding NEPA specifically. (See Chapter 13, "National Environmental Policy Act.")

Advocates should also be conscious of laws controlling other federal agencies (such as the Federal Communications Commission, which has jurisdiction over siting telecommunications facilities) and state agencies, where such laws apply to your particular situation.

Copies of laws and regulations can be easily obtained from the relevant agencies. Always inquire about the existence of other documents or written agency policy statements concerning protecting national parks or significant public natural and cultural resources. Using an agency's own policy statements to argue against a proposed action by that agency can be an extremely effective technique.

How to Fight External Threats

One of the first things park advocates must recognize is that, unfortunately, in many ways American society is poorly equipped to protect parks from harmful activities arising outside their borders. American society is based on free-market principles and private property rights. It has built-in obstacles to complicated, cooperative management of resources across sociopolitical boundaries.

Often, the most significant obstacle to effectively protecting parks is not lack of scientific evidence, or lack of legal principles, but an inability to successfully challenge predominant economic forces and to muster the necessary political will to act decisively.

But American society is changing. Responding to transboundary issues is now a key frontier of park protection. Since there is no "silver bullet" strategy that will automatically avert a major park threat, the effective park defender combines legal tools found in federal, state and local law with strong public involvement and targeted political activity. Exercising creativity and using a variety of approaches from "carrot" to "stick" techniques are the keys to success.

Each situation demands a unique game plan. Nonetheless, park advocates should follow some general guidelines when grappling with external threat issues:

•Establish clear objectives.

Protecting parks first requires an understanding of what you are protecting. Identify specific park values that are distinctive, precious and most important to the health of the park. Then identify the values at risk from an adjacent activity. Wildlife migration routes? Solitude and silence inside the park? The setting around a historic structure? The purity of park air or water?

It may also be useful to approach activities outside the parks in the context of your ideal "vision" for the management of the park and its related lands in the local or regional setting. Try to define that vision. What types of activities around your park would be acceptable or definitely incompatible? How do you see the park functioning in terms of serving and dealing with visitors, interacting with local communities, and acting as a component of the regional economy?

Once you have attempted to answer some of these questions, you can begin to work toward that vision, instead of just reacting to events. Connect your ends—land-use objectives near parks—with specific means. In addition, thinking through these issues may help you to evaluate to what degree an activity might impair park values and to what extent you must be concerned. If the activity, in virtually any form, is clearly incompatible with your vision for the park, your objective might be to stop it outright, instead of attempting to mitigate effects.

•Avert potential threats through cooperative planning.

There are a number of major areas in which you can work positively to avert park threats. One of the most important ways is to promote cooperative/integrated land-use planning.

The best defense is a good offense. It is much easier, and places park resources at less risk, to emphasize sensitive planning and compatible activities on adjacent lands rather than to resolve controversial issues piecemeal. Once an idea or plan for potentially park-damaging activity gets off the ground and gains momentum, the fight against it may be mostly uphill.

Get involved early in planning and land-use decisions for public and private lands adjacent to the parks. Concentrate on averting adjacent land-use problems. Stay alert for potential problems, and act quickly to divert or stop them. Get on mailing lists for the parks, forests and other agencies in your area to keep up-to-date on agency activities. Many national forests, for example, publish regular planning updates that list the projects and their status.

Work with land managers on park issues and promote park protection up front. This may mean commenting on a plan for an adjacent national forest or Bureau of Land Management area, participating in zoning decisions at the local level or interacting directly with landowners next to the park. Ask for what you believe is necessary to protect your park and be persistent. Be pre-

Profile: Molly Schultz

In most respects, 18-year-old Molly Schultz seems like any other bright student headed for college: She's anxious about her future. She'd like to travel and see the world, make a little more money and spend more time hanging out with her friends. But there is plenty to distinguish Schultz from most of her peers. As she prepares to attend Ohio's Antioch College in the fall and work toward a degree in women's studies, Schultz leaves behind more environmental work as a Minneapolis teenager than most people could claim in a lifetime. She has joined volunteer efforts—leafleting and phone canvassing—to save the Canadian rainforest, got involved in planning and research to fight a proposed nuclear waste dump, and now is helping the local Sierra Club research their effort to stop a proposed snowmobile highway through Voyageurs National Park in Minnesota.

She has been to as many environmental demonstrations, it seems, as parties, and even graduated early from high school so she could put in more hours as a phone canvasser for various environmental groups. "But I promised my parents," she says, "that I wouldn't get arrested until I was 18."

So far, so good. Schultz has bigger goals: She'd like to teach, and that is what drives her work for environmental causes, whether it involves giving a talk to fourth graders on recycling, starting up her own student environmental group, or donning "Ozone Alert" signs and a radiation suit in a shopping mall, speaking to passersby about ways to plug up the hole in the ozone. "I try to turn these conflicts that I'm involved in into education opportunities rather than confrontation," she says.

Her student group, for example, was called ECOS (Environmental Coalition of Students), and brought together a dozen or so students from eight different local high schools who, like Schultz, "wanted to change the world, but weren't really sure how to do it." Without funding or even a regular space to meet, Schultz had ECOS holding informational talks with students at local schools and distributing information in shopping malls and in the community about such issues as rainforest destruction and ozone depletion. The group disbanded after several months, but Schultz says, "we got to educate ourselves about environmental issues. It was a real catalyst. And it was fun."

Schultz went on to do volunteer work for the Rainforest Action Network, the Sierra Club, Citizens for a Better Environment, and a handful of local environmental causes. As she gets ready for school in the fall, Schultz is still working about 20 hours a week as an unpaid volunteer for these groups. And her paid work? Molly works in a local health food store and gets paid to do phone canvassing for yet another environmental cause.

She proudly credits her activist drive to what she calls her "hippie" upbringing on an organic farm in Wisconsin. When there wasn't harvesting and other farm chores to do, Schultz spent time roaming the hillsides with her brother, playing in the outdoors. The family's black-and-white TV, Schultz recalls, was hauled out just once a year for *The Wizard of Oz*. Her appreciation of the environment, she says, was borne of idle hours sitting in a lilac tree outside her bedroom window, "just hanging out." When her family moved north to Minneapolis, getting involved in environmental causes seemed natural.

Now she's getting ready for school and eyeing a career in teaching. Still, Schultz has no plans to let up on her environmental work in the meantime. "I'd like to settle down," she says with a long pause, then laughs, "maybe when I'm fifty."

pared to offer alternatives to the proposed action in addition to just opposing it outright. However, in some cases, few "positive" alternatives may exist, and it may be your job to oppose or defeat a project, period.

Park advocates must be prepared to urge the National Park Service to get involved in issues beyond its boundaries and to support NPS when it does. One effective strategy for doing so is to make sure that NPS includes discussion of external threats in planning and park management documents and commits itself to taking action when they arise. NPCA has been successful, for example, in including specific statements about the intent of NPS to confront external threats in the recently revised general management plan for Arches National Park in Utah.

Help encourage constructive dialogue. This responsibility may require substantial effort to educate and sensitize relevant officials, landowners and the public about the concerns and needs of the park. In short, it requires cooperation, collaboration, information sharing and the establishment of formal, lasting relationships among major players in the park's region.

The National Park Service has participated in cooperative efforts, both formally and informally, in various parks around the system. For example, it helped establish the Greater Yellowstone Coordinating Committee in the mid-1980s to integrate planning and decision-making among the two national parks and six national forests in the Yellowstone area. Find out exactly how the staff of your park works with other agencies in the region and consider how that process could be improved.

In addition to "process" strategies—such as consultation—establishing other mechanisms that continually work to protect parks is an efficient strategy in the long run. Some strategies include:

- Instituting local building codes that emphasize protection of aesthetic values and require use of natural materials and native plants for landscaping on lands adjacent to parks. Sensitive building practices can reduce visual intrusions and resource depletion (such as use of water and energy), and limit the spread of nonnative plants and animals.

- Encouraging special protective designations for federal lands adjacent to parks (such as a designation as a wilderness area or BLM "Area of Critical Environmental Concern"). Also, certain uses on adjacent federal lands can be limited to avoid park impacts (such as areas of no timber harvest, off-highway vehicle use restrictions or temporary closures).
- Knowing and using local zoning codes and ordinances. Local laws may influence certain private practices to protect nearby park resources, such as requiring careful food storage and garbage disposal in areas frequented by bears and other park animals.
- Establishing cooperative voluntary arrangements with adjacent landowners. Encourage the donation of "easements" to protect a park's setting. It may benefit both the landowner and the park. An easement is a legal agreement a landowner makes to restrict the type and amount of development that may take place on his or her property.

For parks bordered principally by private or other nonfederal lands, in both urban and rural settings, you should become familiar with the realm of "growth management" strategies. As the nation grapples with the effects of population growth and economic development, people are seeking ways to both maintain the quality of life in their communities—preserving the features that make them special—and support sustainable economic activity.

Park advocates may wish to pursue strategies that attempt to establish a given area outside of a park as a zone of influence or area of concern. Although there has been discussion of the concept, only the legislation establishing Santa Monica Mountains National Recreation Area and the effort to protect the Greater Yellowstone Ecosystem have come close to identifying such areas.

Perhaps the closest existing concept to the "area of concern," although it covers only a narrow segment of the units of the park system, is the International Biosphere Reserve (IBR), a designation of the United Nations Educational, Scientific, and

Cultural Organization (UNESCO). The IBR designation has been applied to 29 units of the system, and in several instances it extends beyond park boundaries to include adjacent (not necessarily contiguous) federal, state and private lands. Essentially, the concept provides for in-depth scientific study and coordinated management of the designated area, with the park serving as a "core" protected area. You may wish to explore how the IBR Program might help your park.

•Understand the potential threats to your park's resources.

Often, a major problem in confronting external threats is the lack of information on park resources and how they might be affected by outside forces. In the absence of solid information, the burden of proof that degradation will result is often left on park advocates, rather than project proponents having to prove that no degradation will occur.

While the National Park Service should conduct a thorough, ongoing program of collecting basic information about park resources and monitoring their condition, it often does not. In fact, the *State of the Parks* report concluded that NPS was suffering from a grave information gap that left 75 percent of the threats reported in 1980 inadequately documented and poorly understood. Enormous needs were identified for monitoring and research to better understand park resources, the forces acting on them, and how to protect them.

Know the basic research needs of your park. Evaluate the existing resource inventory and monitoring program and identify places for improvement. For example, parks located in arid environments, where water is a key limiting factor affecting ecology, should have surveys of existing springs and seeps and groundwater studies that establish basic hydrological information about the park. Such data could be critical in evaluating potential projects outside the park that require water. Work with the Park Service in any way possible to develop guidelines for monitoring and reporting the condition of natural and cultural resources in your park.

Similarly, understanding your park's visitors can be a key factor in addressing external threats. Surveys can establish visitor preferences and concerns, such as outstanding visibility or natural quiet, that NPS should strive to protect. Such work may also include a boundary study to determine the adequacy of the park's boundary with respect to preserving the prime resources that the park was established to protect. (See Chapter 6, "Adjusting Park Boundaries.")

There is no substitute for solid data and scientific evidence about the impacts of a proposed project. One of the most important tools the park advocate has is the National Environmental Policy Act (NEPA), which requires full analysis and disclosure of the impacts of "major federal actions" on the environment. Several states have similar statutes. Demand rigorous analysis of the impacts of the proposed project. If an environmental assessment (EA) prepared under NEPA is not adequate, request preparation of a full environmental impact statement (EIS).

During preparation of an EA or EIS for a project outside park boundaries, it will again be essential that the Park Service be adequately and substantively involved, and park advocates may need to work with NPS to assure that this happens. Or consider getting your own experts to bring new information to bear on the proposed project.

•Communicate effectively and maintain credibility.

Park advocates must recognize that park protection issues are inherently political. Gather adequate information and, where relevant laws are applicable, demand full analysis of a proposed project's impact on your park. Make sure you understand the situation before taking a public position. In short, look before you leap. Ignorance never settles a question.

Pick your fights strategically. Decide whether the problem should be defeated outright or mitigated. In some situations, an immediate response to a potentially damaging project is required, but your cause will not be well-served by knee-jerk reactions that later prove false and erode your credibility. However, strong positions taken early may be essential to head off bad ideas.

Above all, you should work to maintain your stature as a credible resource for agencies, public officials and the public. Know the decision-making process and the key decision-makers. Elected officials are extremely important to most land-use decisions. Clearly articulate your positions, and give officials good reasons (legal, political, economic, moral) to support you by presenting accurate information.

Work to build public support for your park through education. Use the media and other mechanisms to bring public attention to external threats. Organize supporters of the park and seek out new alliances. Whenever possible, stress the benefits of the parks and the importance of maintaining those benefits by protecting the park from harmful activities.

•Fashion a well-organized campaign to protect your park.
Target the enemy. A campaign directed against a single offending party or project, if possible, helps you focus and is easier to understand. Realize that in any effort on behalf of a park, it may take months or years for development proposals to work their way through review and approval phases. Your staying power is crucial.

Strategies may vary depending on the nature and severity of the threat. For example, in fighting the proposed movie theater and commercial complex next to Zion National Park, NPCA used a variety of approaches at different levels. First, it organized letter-writing campaigns to town officials, the Secretary of the Interior and Congress, and promoted stories about the threat in the media. Next it lodged protests and appeals of Springdale town council zoning decisions and explored compromises to resolve the problem. Finally, it filed a formal lawsuit challenging the town council's actions in approving the development.

Two basic paths confront park advocates in protecting parks. The first is one that recognizes that fashioning and implementing good-neighbor policies represents the best hope. Great opportunities lie in cooperative strategies among government agencies and between government and the private sector.

The second path is the sober realization that park advocates often are the last line of defense. Park supporters must step into the breach when government hesitates, and demand rigorous compliance with law and administrative policy to enforce park protections. Holding the line can often improve the chances that cooperative strategies will work better.

Chapter 6

Adjusting Park Boundaries

There is a pleasure in the pathless woods,
There is a rapture on the lonely shore,
There is society, where none intrudes,
By the deep sea and music in its roar:
I love not man the less, but Nature more,
From these our interviews, in which I steal
From all I may be, or have been before,
To mingle with the Universe, and feel
What I can ne'er express, yet cannot all conceal.

Lord Byron

ADJUSTING PARK BOUNDARIES

In 1933, when Congress set aside 80,000 acres of Sonoran desert filled with lanky saguaro cacti as Saguaro National Monument, Tucson's outer limits were 15 miles from the park's borders and its population was 35,000. The past 60 years have seen Tucson grow to a bustling metropolis of 675,000 people—and it continues to grow at a rate of 2.5 percent each year.

Today, Tucson's city border has edged to within a mile of Saguaro. It may move even closer if developers of a resort community are allowed to build on their proposed site near Saguaro's eastern border—a mere 50 feet from the monument. With Tucson creeping ever closer, will the park's borders actually be able to protect Saguaro's natural resources from the effects of urban sprawl?

The "resource-based" boundary is the single most important factor governing the management and fate of a park. A boundary that adequately encloses and protects the resources being preserved greatly reduces the risk of threat from outside activities. But establishing park borders is never a simple matter.

Where the lines are drawn has broad legal, social and political implications. From the establishment of Yellowstone in 1872 to Great Basin National Park in 1986, the history of the National Park System is replete with boundary-related debates and struggles over both additions and deletions to parks.

For both local communities and the National Park Service,

having a clearly defined boundary is comforting, allowing people to say, "This is my side of the line, that's yours." Fixed boundaries define the limits of where the Park Service may implement regulatory authorities and enforce federal law. Boundary lines also may determine whether the Park Service might be legislatively empowered to enter into cooperative agreements with adjacent landowners.

When boundary changes are discussed, the stakes—and the tensions—may run high; often the choice is between preservation and use, or even the loss of resources, and between competing public and private values. Although there have been hundreds of beneficial park expansions over the years, many adjacent land problems cannot be solved simply with a boundary expansion.

Revising a park boundary is a complex process that must be approached with extreme care. Any adjustment will involve numerous players and will take time and close cooperation, not just with national park officials, but with congressional representatives, state and local government officials and the local community. Because significant boundary changes usually require a change in the enabling legislation for the park, your congressional delegation has a particularly important role. The key roles for the park advocate in initiating a boundary revision are marshaling facts and strong supporting arguments and gaining broad public support for the change. Perseverance, often over several years, is all too often required to achieve results.

Park Boundaries: Problems and Prospects

When the National Park Service was carving out six million-acre Denali National Park in 1980, amid wrangling with native landowners, NPS Alaska Regional Director John Cooke commented, "There are two things you never want to see being made: sausages and boundaries." It's true.

Boundaries are usually the results of political compromise with competing interests, and the final products are often far from perfect. Many times boundary lines do not include significant resources that deserve federal protection. Some boundaries were drawn so long ago that they fail to adequately protect existing park resources. Moreover, the management of dynamic resources, such as wildlife, which do not recognize artificially drawn, inflexible boundaries, presents a great challenge.

Establishing sound, resource-based boundaries that fully protect the parks has been a problem from the earliest days of the National Park System. Because the notion of "ecosystem management" didn't exist in the late 1800s, neither the Yosemite nor the Yellowstone park acts adequately provided for the preservation of these outstanding areas in perpetuity. For example, the laws fail to protect the watersheds that feed the Yosemite Valley's magnificent waterfalls, the sweeping views from the Sierra mountain crests, or even the full diversity of wildlife habitats that define the area's wild character.

The boundary of Yellowstone is a virtual square—a cookie-cutter corner of Wyoming (including tiny strips of Montana and Idaho) that slices across mountain ranges, watersheds and wildlife habitat. It is not large enough to ensure ironclad protection for the area's world-class thermal features. Critical winter range for elk and bison, and much of the prime habitat of the threatened grizzly bear, remain outside the park.

The preservation of scenic features embodied in the Yosemite and Yellowstone enabling acts demonstrates the way the boundaries of many of the first national parks were drawn. Early national park legislation merely sought to mark what was most visually spectacular. Like the frame of an Italian masterpiece, the straight-line boundaries of these parks only enclosed the area's most dramatic features. Ecosystem management or protection had nothing to do with it. Moreover, boundaries were set so as not to jeopardize the economic potential that surrounding lands might hold for agriculture, industry or other development interests.

Today, many large natural national park areas do not incorporate complete ecosystems. They often face diverse types of external threats from energy exploration and production, air and water pollution, construction and development, as well as a host of other threats. Many of today's most pressing park management problems are directly attributable to inadequate park boundaries.

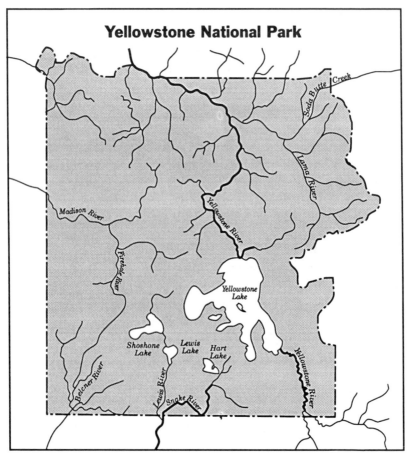

Framing a masterpiece: The straight-line boundaries of the first national parks, like Yellowstone, tried to frame the areas' most dramatic features, often ignoring the larger ecosystem and surrounding lands.

Similarly, the boundaries of many historic units in the National Park System have been drawn to encompass only areas perceived as the sites of significant human activity. Other boundaries simply failed to include lands later deemed important because of archaeological or historical information which were unknown at the time. In addition, particularly in historic and cultural areas, borders were drawn without any attempt to preserve historic scenes, settings or vistas, which today are considered essential components of the cultural landscape.

For many Civil War battlefields, for example, broader protections did not seem necessary since nearly all such battles were fought in what were at the time rural areas; few people could have envisioned the encroachment of suburban sprawl on these areas. Yet today, there is hardly a Civil War battlefield in the eastern United States that is not threatened by residential or commercial development.

Unfortunately, politics more often than not play an important role in drawing boundary lines. For example, at Great Basin National Park, one of the nation's newest national parks (established in 1986), the original boundary proposals were dramatically reduced so that lands that held potential for mining, hunting and grazing in the area would not be jeopardized. So we're left with an ironic result: There is no actual "basin" preserved in Great Basin National Park.

Despite directives from Congress to prepare a comprehensive study of the adequacy of national park boundaries, the National Park Service has never comprehensively done so.

Today, boundary revisions are made on a park-by-park basis and are usually identified in a park's general management plan, statement for management or land protection plan. Thousands of potential adjustments have been discussed by the National Park Service, Congress, private organizations and individuals over the years. To date, more than 500 boundary revisions have been authorized for nearly 200 parks. Though many of the adjustments have been relatively minor in size, most of them, especially in the last 20 years, have incorporated significant resources that previously were outside park boundaries.

Some expansions have been sizable. These often accompany a change in designation. For example, Congress recently expanded Fort Jefferson National Monument off the coast of Florida by 64,000 acres and redesignated it Dry Tortugas National Park.

Adjusting Park Boundaries

Boundary adjustments to national parks can be authorized by the President, the Secretary of the Interior or Congress. In most cases, your congressman or senator will be responsible for introducing a boundary revision bill into the legislature, although private citizens often provide the catalyst to force consideration of a boundary change proposal. While the Secretary of the Interior or Congress can initiate a boundary revision on their own, citizen action has been far and away the most important force in establishing, protecting and expanding parks.

You should be familiar with all of the options and steps involved in the boundary modification process. Strategies must be developed for each of these stages in order to successfully influence the outcome. For example, a typical boundary modification proposal might follow a process over several years that would include:

1—Development of a constituency seeking to revise the park's boundary;

2—Development of a "boundary concept" proposal in conjunction with park officials, local officials and activists, and members of Congress (often this is suggested in a park's general management plan or land protection plan);

3—Completion of a formal, professional study of the proposal (this is desirable but not mandatory);

4—Administrative action or development of legislation to implement the change;

5—A one- to two-year effort to turn the boundary revision proposal into public law.

Although most boundary revisions take several years to accomplish, "emergency" acquisitions can and do occur. Some parks have a special provision written into their enabling legislation that permits a boundary adjustment merely by publishing a notice in the *Federal Register.* Also, if the boundary revision is deemed a "minor boundary adjustment," no legislation may be necessary.

You also must remember that the National Park Service, though a preservation agency, is a ponderous, conservative bureau within the Department of the Interior. High-level Department of Interior or NPS officials may initially oppose measures that park superintendents or professional staff think are in a park's best interest. Historically, many Interior and Park Service political appointees have opposed new park proposals and failed to support boundary expansions. Keep in mind that Congress, not NPS, enacts boundary revisions. Although it is best to have the support of the agency, it will not always be possible.

Within the last decade, the National Park Service has begun to move away from general support of park boundary expansion to general opposition, in an effort to satisfy the budget concerns at the Office of Management and Budget (OMB), an agency whose sole purpose is to keep government spending down. You should remember that the politics of Congress and the Department of the Interior may also play a major role in helping or hindering NPS's ability to make professional recommendations regarding park boundaries.

Is a Boundary Change Really Necessary?

Boundary changes at parks are often necessary, desirable and, in many cases, politically feasible. In other cases, boundary changes may not be essential or sensible. And sometimes, even adjusting boundaries might not be the best method to ensure adequate protection for park resources.

A decision to change a park boundary is a serious matter. There are issues that you must examine closely before determining a proper course of action. For example, when confronted with problems (such as an external park threat) or with opportunities (such as adjacent land becoming available), early consultation with other conservationists at the local and national levels is usually important.

Are the Resources Significant?

When evaluating a course of action for a proposed boundary modification, you should consider the standards and policies of the National Park Service. The official policies of the National Park Service regarding boundary expansions are contained in several important documents which you can obtain from NPS regional offices.

The first is a short pamphlet called "Criteria for Parkland." Boundary expansion proposals are measured against the same criteria used to evaluate proposals for new parks: 1) the *significance* of the resources to be incorporated; 2) their *suitability* for inclusion in the National Park System; and 3) the *feasibility* of managing the area.

In order to evaluate a boundary proposal, the National Park Service requires submission of:

- an analysis of whether the existing boundary provides for the adequate protection and preservation of the natural, historic, cultural, scenic and recreational resources integral to the park;
- an evaluation of each parcel proposed for addition or deletion based on this analysis;
- and an assessment of the effect of potential boundary adjustments, taking into consideration the factors listed above as well as the effect of the adjustments on the local communities and surrounding areas.

The law also requires that in proposing any boundary changes, the Secretary of the Interior also shall "consult with affected agencies of state and local governments, surrounding communities, affected landowners and private, national, regional and local organizations." Further, an estimate of the cost of the acquisition, an explanation of the basis for the estimate, and a statement on the "relative priority" of the acquisition within the National Park System as a whole must be submitted.

It is important for you to understand these criteria and how they might be applied. The professional opinion of the National Park Service is often a key factor in public debate and one that Congress looks to for guidance. You must be prepared to rigorously defend a boundary change proposal and, if need be, challenge the findings of the Park Service if they are inaccurate or appear to have been politically manipulated.

What Other Factors and Options Must be Considered?

Choosing the proper political approach to achieving a boundary revision depends on the unique circumstances at each park. In addition to evaluating the significance of the resources involved, there are other key questions to consider:

•What existing laws are applicable to the situation?

You should obtain a copy of the enabling legislation for your park and understand all possibilities and restrictions on land acquisition and boundary changes. Find out if there are any special authorities or conditions on land acquisition contained in the park's enabling legislation.

Congress has established various strategies for park protection and land acquisition. You may want to compare, for example, approaches taken at other similar parks. In many Civil War national military parks, like Chickamauga and Chattanooga National Military Park (as well as in most of the older, large natural area parks), the federal government sought to own most of the significant battle lands from the start. In contrast, at Antietam National Battlefield, and many of the other units designated as national battlefields, a small land base with scenic easements was the original preferred protection mechanism. (This approach, known as the "Antietam Plan," in many cases has proved insufficient to defend park values. Congress continues to expand the park boundaries at many battlefield areas.)

More recently, at Richmond National Battlefield Park, Congress authorized the National Park Service to purchase any lands it considered important to historic or scenic protection within five miles of existing battlefields. In the course of expanding the boundaries of Fredericksburg and Spotsylvania National Military Park and Gettysburg National Military Park to include significant lands, Congress took the creative step of authorizing NPS to accept donations of easements on lands adjacent to the park or within a designated historic preservation and conservation zone. These recent approaches give NPS greater flexibility, and the ability to respond to opportunities to protect parks, without the necessity of passing yet another formal boundary expansion.

•Are there willing sellers involved? Would "condemnation" of private lands be required?

The enabling legislation for some parks specifically prohibits acquisition of lands without the consent of the owner. In some circumstances, NPS is prohibited from accepting lands other than by donation. At other parks, the Park Service may possess the authority of eminent domain, which allows the government to initiate a very formal process of appraisal and adjudicated settlement, even over the objections of landowners. The process is commonly known as "condemnation."

A boundary expansion involving willing sellers or donations usually garners little community or political opposition. It is well worth trying to obtain owner consent *prior* to moving forward too far with a boundary proposal. If owners reject federal efforts to buy the land, other land-protection tools exist, such as easements or purchase by private organizations and land trusts. Often these alternative tools are attractive to landowners because of tax breaks that can accrue to the owner.

•Are there alternatives to a boundary change?

Consider the alternatives to acquisition and how would they be effective in meeting your park protection goals. It is not necessary or desirable for the National Park Service to control or manage every acre adjacent to or important to a park. Various laws require other federal agencies managing lands adjacent to parks, such as the Bureau of Land Management or U.S. Forest Service, to take the needs of adjacent park resources into account in their decision-making. In this case, citizen efforts to force compliance with existing laws, or to implement cooperative agreements and better coordination between these agencies and NPS, can be very effective and may obviate the need for a formal park boundary expansion.

Similarly, on adjacent public or private lands, NPS or private interests might employ appropriate tools, funds and expertise (if available) to assist local governments and landowners in developing land-use strategies that are compatible with park needs.

Legislative Authorities and Processes

Many laws apply when initiating and achieving a boundary modification. Successful efforts combine administrative, legal and citizen-action measures into an effective strategy.

•Antiquities Act

Under the 1906 Antiquities Act, the President has the authority to declare national monuments comprised of existing federal lands. Although this authority has been used in the past to establish national monuments, rather than enlarge existing ones, it remains an option worthy of consideration. Because this type of action does not require the approval of Congress, it can be the boldest, shortest route to a desired end, though not necessarily the easiest route.

Usually, the land must be in federal ownership or the property owner must be willing to donate the land to the park. Significant political support would need to be exercised, and an area must face extremely serious and imminent threats in order to motivate the executive branch to accept the property.

•Planning Process and Minor Boundary Adjustment

Although the National Park Service has never reviewed park boundaries in a systematic manner, a public law requires NPS to consider "indications of potential modifications to the external boundaries of the unit, and the reasons therefore" in the preparation of all park general management plans.

Every park is supposed to have an approved general management plan. This document sets forth a management concept for the park within a local and regional context and maps strategies for achieving park objectives for resource protection and visitor use. The plan is normally reviewed every 10 to 15 years and this review process is a key opportunity for you to raise boundary modification issues.

The National Park Service has the authority to make minor boundary revisions under a 1977 amendment to the Land and Water Conservation Act. This authority was granted to NPS mainly to deal with land donation offers, but money appropriated by Congress under the act can be used to acquire lands included in minor boundary revisions. Congress, however, restricted this boundary adjustment authority in several ways. Adjustments may be made only to parks established after January 1, 1965, and must be preceded by notice to the appropriate committees in Congress, publication of a revised boundary map or other description in the *Federal Register,* and consultation with local authorities and the local public. Additionally, NPS may not acquire property in these circumstances without the consent of the owner, any publicly owned lands must be donated, and the Secretary may not exchange any existing parkland for other lands.

•Special Studies

It is common for a special boundary study to be initiated by a park superintendent, a National Park Service regional office or a citizen. For particularly large or controversial proposals, you may prefer to talk with your park's superintendent to consider whether it would be more appropriate for NPS or Congress to initiate a boundary study. Yet another option is to examine the possibility of getting NPS to start work on an "adjacent lands study," which evaluates the overall park setting within its surroundings. Funds for such studies usually need to be directed from the existing NPS budget, although citizens groups often are able to raise "seed money" to initiate a study while additional federal funds are being secured.

•Congress and the Legislative Process

The route most commonly followed to achieve boundary modifications is through Congress. This is often a tortuous and complicated path and does not always lead to success. If the U.S. representative whose district includes the park areas is supportive and if one of the state's two U.S. senators supports the proposal, you may have a good chance of winning. You must be diligent in involving the congressional delegation in the process. Involve them early and keep them involved in bill drafting, grassroots coordination, and finally, lobbying for enactment. Keep in mind that boundary legislation must pass both the Senate and House of Representatives in identical form before it can be signed by the President.

Congressional subcommittees with responsibility for oversight of the national parks normally prefer to have formal studies completed for boundary modifications prior to considering specific legislation. A completed study can dramatically increase prospects for success. When a proposal is ripe for action and legislation has been prepared, co-sponsors should be recruited, usually from the state's delegation. A large list of bipartisan co-sponsors tells other members of Congress that this is a bill worth supporting and that it is not a partisan issue.

If park boundary proposals are important enough to be introduced in Congress, you and your key congressional supporters must make the commitment to pressure sponsors and key committee chairs to hold hearings and act on the legislation.

It should be noted that during the hearing process, the Administration will present a formal opinion on legislation. The testimony must clear the Office of Management and Budget, which determines the legislation's effect on the federal budget and its consistency with the President's overall program. Also, before a vote on legislation, the Congressional Budget Office must prepare an estimate of the costs involved. At each of these junctures, you may need to bring pressure to bear or counter negative opinions about your proposal.

Assuming the bill is enacted, the work on the park boundary modification necessarily does not end. The boundary may be authorized, but funds may need to be "appropriated" to purchase the lands. This may require you to be actively involved in the annual congressional budget process to secure Land and Water Conservation Fund monies for the park. Again, working in coalitions as closely as possible with your congressional delegation is a good recipe for success.

How You Can Achieve Boundary Adjustments

•**Know your park well.** Familiarize yourself with the park's resources, their relationship to surrounding lands, and the physical boundaries of the park. Learn about the management of the park and any particular transboundary problems that are present or may occur in the future. Where a park is surrounded by other federal or public lands, make the effort to reach out to other land managers to better understand their perspectives and how they interact with the park.

•**Obtain and review your park's various plans.** In particular, review the statement for management, the general management plan and the land protection plan. Note any sections that discuss land acquisition, adjacent lands, future threats or concerns about effective park administration that may be facilitated by, or require, a boundary expansion. Learn about any existing land-acquisition priorities for your park.

•**Watch for any project or activity on adjacent lands that might affect the park.** Boundary expansions are not the only solutions to problems, many of which can be averted by effective citizen action to stop or mitigate threatening activities.

•**Respect the property rights of adjacent landowners at all times.** This includes other public land agencies. Do not trespass or survey private lands without the owner's consent. In any outreach efforts, treat all landowners with respect. Listen and try to respond to their concerns with accurate information. Keep in mind that any successful boundary modification must have the support of a majority of landowners as well as the community.

•**Be alert for opportunities.** Boundary adjustments that appear unlikely at one point may become possible as social, political and economic conditions change.

Park additions may be easier when land is undergoing a change in ownership, when tax codes or economic conditions favor preservation over development (as during a recession), or when Congress is considering any other legislation affecting the park or the area.

•**Develop only strong proposals.** Your proposals should undergo rigorous review and analysis of their significance and feasibility. Make contact with resource professionals—at nearby universities and/or field stations—to stay abreast of current research on the park and its setting (such as research on wildlife migration or new archaeological discoveries or historical information that bears on the park).

•**Identify the key players.** This means all of them—friends and foes. Think creatively about coalition building. Where it's appropriate and possible, involve local commercial and tourism interests, federal and local governments and agencies, landowners, politicians, development interests and various user groups.

•**Iron out as many problems as possible before taking a proposal to Congress.** The road to congressional approval is arduous. Have all the facts and understand the issues before you begin to gather the necessary congressional support.

•**Pursue your goals aggressively.** Combine legislative, media, grassroots and other measures into an effective overall strategy.

Chapter 7

Inholdings: Private Lands Within Parks

There is no better service we can render to the masses of the people than to set about and preserve for them wide space of fine scenery for their delight.

James Bryce

INHOLDINGS: PRIVATE LANDS WITHIN PARKS

Imagine an RV park with several hundred sites...deep in the heart of Alaska's pristine Denali National Park. One developer can—she first proposed the idea back in 1990 and continues to push for it. Currently, the only traffic on Denali's one steep, windy dirt road is a limited number of park shuttle buses, each carrying only 40 passengers, reducing the risk of accidents and increasing visitors' opportunities to view Denali's spectacular wildlife: caribou, grizzlies, wolves, moose and more than 150 species of birds. How will scores of 24-foot motor homes roving daily across the park affect this subarctic wildlife sanctuary? It's anybody's guess. You ask, "How could the Park Service let her build within the park?" Simple. *It's her land.*

A common, and dangerous, public misperception surrounding national parks is that once a park area is designated by Congress, all the land within its boundaries is protected automatically. Although many parks were carved out of extensive tracts of public land and are fully owned and managed by the federal government, many others have more complicated land-ownership patterns. In these cases, the authorized boundaries may include nonfederal lands, over which the National Park Service's authority is limited. Nonfederal lands owned by private entities, state or local governments, or in some cases Native American corporations, are generally known as "inholdings."

Currently about two million acres of private lands are contained within the National Park System, many based on mining and homesteading claims. While their owners may leave them undisturbed and undeveloped for decades, each poses a potential threat to its surrounding park. It is up to you to know your park's inholdings and plan cooperatively to ensure that activity on the private land is consistent with your park's resource protection goals. In instances where a direct threat exists, you may need to take steps to help acquire an inholding for the park.

Many Parks Have Many Owners

National parks show a full range of ownership patterns. At one end of the spectrum are areas such as Cuyahoga Valley National Recreation Area, Cape Cod National Seashore and Santa Monica Mountains National Recreation Area, designated with the understanding that the entire park area would never be fully federally owned. Although less than half the acreage within Cuyahoga's boundary is under federal ownership, the various local jurisdictions involved were part of the development process and part of multi-jurisdictional, comprehensive planning for the valley. Although Cuyahoga faces many problems, the challenge of managing an area with multiple owners was recognized in its designation. At the other end of the spectrum is a park like Craters of the Moon National Monument, whose 53,500 acres are wholly owned by the federal government. The surprising truth, however, is that national parks, including the oldest "crown jewel" parks, do contain private lands. Even the first national park, Yellowstone, still contains 18 acres of nonfederal land.

Inholdings come in many sizes, have various types of owners, and present varying threats to the integrity of a park. Landowners may include individuals, estates or trusts, private corporations, or even states or local governments. Many Western states, for example, were granted lands that eventually wound up within the boundaries of national parks. National park inholdings may be bought and sold freely on the open market, like other forms of real estate, without the involvement or consent of the Park Service.

Parks with areas, even relatively small areas, of nonfederal land face resource protection challenges and serious threats. Denali National Park, a 4.7 million-acre wilderness park in central Alaska, is 99.9 percent federally owned. Many of the more than 4,000 acres of private land in the park, however, are located in places that are key activity zones where private actions (such as the proposed RV park in Denali) could have far-reaching consequences for park management and resource protection.

A number of inholdings can be traced to mining claims. The now-antiquated General Mining Law of 1872 granted settlers almost limitless rights to mineral extraction on public lands in order to encourage Western expansion. Although a 1976 congressional act prevented the further patenting of mineral rights in parks, at least 24 national parks (including Death Valley and Organ Pipe Cactus national monuments and Crater Lake National Park) still contain valid mining claims. Today, there are 30,000 acres of private property within Alaskan parks acquired under the 1872 mining law.

At least 24 national parks contain inholdings acquired under the mining law of 1872.

Legally, once lands have been patented, even explicitly for mineral extraction, their owners can do whatever they please with them. In several instances, owners of active claims have sought to develop (or sell their lands to be developed) for tourism after mineral resources were depleted. Mining land in the Kantishna area in the center of Denali has been repeatedly proposed for commercial development. One Kantishna inholder has threatened to shoot anyone who crosses his land and another pair in the area, the Wheeler brothers, have suggested they might bulldoze a gigantic letter "W" on a mountainside within their property line.

Unfortunately, a single inholding in the wrong hands, or put to the wrong uses, can seriously affect an entire park. At times in the past, efforts to avert development on park inholdings have failed, with tragic consequences. In 1972, a 307-foot tourist tower was built on an inholding at Gettysburg National Military Park in Pennsylvania, despite findings by the National Park Service and the Advisory Council on Historic Preservation that the tower would adversely affect the battlefield park, and despite a lawsuit by the state. But even with this directive, reversal of such a scar on a park is an expensive and lengthy process.

Thus, the National Park Service and park advocates must pay particular attention to inholdings, especially those that have lain "dormant" for years. These may suddenly spring to life and present a park protection crisis.

Acquisition of Inholdings

Inholdings present interesting cases with respect to the law and the National Park Service has various steps it can take to address such lands. Acquisition is often the preferred alternative and the course that was envisioned when the park was established. Acquisition authority is stated in the enabling legislation for each park. Enabling language may allow NPS to purchase or condemn land for acquisition, or, as has frequently been the case with newer parks that include private lands, it may permit acquisition only through donation, land exchange or purchase from a willing seller. NPS may also be authorized to spend money on a variety of alternative protection strategies, such as easements, or may be authorized to participate or aid in the development of local land-use plans to protect nonfederal lands within parks.

One of the first critical steps taken by the National Park Service after the designation of a park is the preparation of a Land Protection Plan. This plan details ownership patterns, lays out a framework for protecting park resources through any needed acquisitions, and identifies priority parcels for acquisition. Priorities for land acquisition are first established at the park level, then within the NPS region, and, finally, nationally as part of the President's annual budget for NPS.

Park advocates should understand the dynamics and challenges of national parkland acquisition. Federal funding for inholding acquisition comes from the Land and Water Conservation Fund (LWCF), revenues which are derived from royalties on offshore oil and gas leasing and other sources. Although $900 million is credited annually to the fund and is available for Congress to appropriate to federal land management agencies for land acquisition, in recent years much less than that has actually been appropriated. Over the past decade, LWCF appropriations have averaged only about 30 percent of the $900 million potentially available each year. With substantial needs for land acquisition not only across the National Park System, but also in national wildlife refuges, national forests and other public lands, competition for these funds is stiff.

The proposed budget for the National Park Service usually contains a list of land acquisition projects for which the agency seeks funding. Congress, however, reviews and modifies this final list, distributing available LWCF revenues based on their own views about federal spending, park resource protection and other political considerations. Land acquisition is one of the line items in the NPS budget over which Congress has the greatest influence. Park advocates seeking land-acquisition funds must therefore pull out all the stops to support their priority projects. This requires extensive work to build a case for funding the acquisition and to create political coalitions to back the project. Close coordination with congressional offices and conservationist allies is essential throughout the annual funding appropriations cycle and beyond. (See Chapter 14, "Congress and the National Parks.") Even after funds have been appropriated for acquisition, a good deal of time may pass before an inholding is actually acquired because NPS must complete appraisal, negotiations and purchase agreements.

Park advocates also frequently help the National Park Service directly with land acquisition. Recent years have seen an increase in both the number and the activity of organizations working to acquire and protect national parklands, either for resale to NPS or for outright donation. The expertise of such organizations is immensely valuable to NPS and park advocates. Nonprofit land trusts can respond more quickly than the government, and their involvement can frequently result in lower acquisition costs. (Some of the leading organizations working to obtain national park inholdings are listed in Additional Resources, pg. 197.)

Protection Without Purchase

The Organic Act established the standard by which the Secretary of the Interior (and NPS) must manage parks. It provides general regulatory authority over parklands and activities occurring on them. Past Secretaries have used this authority to regulate such diverse matters as backcountry travel, boating, fire management and snowmobile use. They have also created regulations limiting activities occurring on nonfederal lands located within the national parks. The courts have consistently sustained these uses of the Secretary's authority as long as there is a reasonable connection between the regulation and the preservation-enjoyment mandate of the Organic Act. Thus, to the extent that threats to park resources involve internal activities by inholders, the Secretary has considerable legal authority under the Organic Act to respond and limit access or use. There may also be state or local statutes that affect land use or transfers of inholdings.

Land acquisition, either by the federal government or by private citizens on behalf of the parks, can be extremely contentious and volatile local and national issues. Private land and the freedoms that accompany land ownership are a cornerstone of American democracy, and opinions on private rights to retain and use land are strongly held in this country.

These feelings may be even stronger where parks are concerned. Many private landowners, as well as state and local owners of inholdings, view their lands as valuable treasures. For some, the thought of giving up land, even for fair compensation or to meet broad public values, or of having the federal government hinder in any way what they might choose to do with their land, is intolerable. In situations in which park designations were opposed by local landowners, such emotions may translate into years of controversy over NPS land-acquisition programs.

Frequently, emotions run highest over the use of eminent domain (or condemnation) authority by the National Park Service. It is important to recognize that in some situations, land-acquisition programs have been problematic, and condemnation authority has been wielded clumsily by NPS in the past. However, it is equally important to recognize that eminent domain authority, used sparingly, in some cases actually can be employed as an advantage to the landowner. Condemnation provides certain legal protections and advantages to the landowner which would be denied in a normal negotiated purchase.

At least one national organization, the National Inholders Association, serves as a voice for inholders on federal lands and is a frequent critic of land acquisition by the National Park Service. Park advocates are wise to become familiar with this organization's tactics, which frequently distort facts and are designed to be disruptive to parkland acquisition and resource protection.

What You Can Do About Inholdings

•**Determine the degree to which inholdings play a significant role in your park**. This will depend on three main factors: the amount of nonfederal land within the park's boundaries; the degree of control your park management has over acquisition according to its enabling legislation; and the potential for resource degradation.

The first two questions can be answered by talking with your park superintendent. Ask for a copy of the general management plan and land protection plan. The superintendent can tell you the policies and regulations governing inholdings for the park and give you a copy of the enabling legislation, which will de-

Profile: Anne Wieland

On a bright winter morning, Anne Wieland sits out near the back porch of her bayfront home in Hope, Alaska, watching a pack of sea otters sunbathe on the ice. There is no central heating or plumbing here, just the basics—an outhouse and a telephone. But there is also the imposing view across Kachemak Bay: some 23,000 acres of old-growth forest which, until Wieland and a group of volunteers began working to protect it from logging interests several years ago, stood to become a clear-cut wasteland.

A New Jersey native, 60-year-old Wieland first came to Alaska in 1957, on a honeymoon with her husband to Prince William Sound.

The newlyweds happily counted salmon in a fish factory. They settled in Anchorage, eventually, where Wieland began a long teaching career and raised a family. But when the marriage ended years later and her daughters had left home, Wieland feared she was growing old with dreams yet unfulfilled.

"I'd been doing somebody else's work all my life—putting my ex-husband through medical school, raising kids, helping other teachers—and I wanted a life of my own again."

Eleven million gallons of crude, ironically, helped bring it back—and, as Wieland says now, gazing across the bay, "ended up being the very vehicle that saved our state park." When the Exxon *Valdez* spill of 1989 reached the area of Prince William Sound where Wieland had honeymooned, "I was utterly devastated. I had to do something. We were thrown into this and I didn't have time to think, 'I don't know how to do that' or 'I can't do it.' We just did it." Wieland worked as a national hotline coordinator, cleaned oil-soaked otters and joined hundreds of other volunteers in helping to scour the beaches.

That experience drove Wieland into action on the next issue that stared out at her across the bay in Hope. Twenty-three thousand acres of Kachemak forestland, part of inholdings in Kachemak State Park on the Kenai Coast, had been sold to a logging company. For Wieland and 4,000 other summer residents who faced having their state park clear-cut, it was a frightening possibility. "After the tragedy of the oil spill," Wieland says, "the prospect of logging was unthinkable. I wasn't going to stand by and watch it happen."

Wieland brought her organizing and teaching skills out of retirement and joined a small group called the Kachemak Bay Citizens Coalition. She conducted real estate and wildlife surveys of the Kachemak region that would have been impacted by logging—her own version of an environmental impact statement—and she joined other volunteers in an all-out campaign to get the state to buy back the land from the Timber Trading Company.

The effort included letter-writing and telephone campaigns, and the group raised enough donations to place full-page ads in newspapers and to hire a lobbyist to carry the message to the state legislature.

"Little by little, we diversified, we were persistent, and the governor finally saw the light," Wieland recalls. The state bought the land for $22 million—and Exxon, as it turns out, paid for it with an endowment created out of the criminal fines it owed the state as the result of the *Valdez* disaster.

The jubilant Wieland—who splits time these days between her home in Anchorage and her Kachemak cabin, where she kayaks and continues to work as a marine science educator—joined her volunteer comrades on a trip to Anchorage to celebrate with the governor, and for the first time in as long as she could remember, bought a dressy outfit for the occasion. Wieland, who's more at home in jeans and a parka, enjoyed a brief moment of pomp and circumstance. "I'm really a hippie," she admits. "But it was fun."

scribe land acquisition authorities at the park. If your park is actively acquiring land, ask for a list of acquisition priorities and criteria. If the park has inholdings that it cannot acquire, ask for a plan for establishing protection measures for nonfederal areas. If your park has inholdings with resources that are not well-documented, encourage NPS to conduct appropriate studies.

•**Become familiar with and monitor inholdings.** If actions harmful to park resources are proposed, or are taking place, contact the superintendent. Consider the range of actions that might be appropriate as a response. Actions on nonfederal land should not go unquestioned. Regardless of the ownership, the land is still within the boundaries of the National Park System. Alert park supporters and the local public to the threat. Capitalize on the strong public sentiment that exists to see national parks protected.

•**Support the NPS land-acquisition program if appropriate.** If your park has an active land-acquisition program, get involved. Focus on top priority acquisitions, building public and political support for land preservation. Work with your congressional representatives to secure needed funds, and cooperate with non-governmental organizations such as land trusts. Publicize successful land-protection efforts.

•**Develop a consensus among interested parties in protecting lands inside the park.** Work with your community and all levels of government. Be respectful of private property within national parks and work toward establishing good relations between landowners, park supporters and NPS. Where land-ownership patterns are complex, and federal lands are not extensive or are scattered, encourage resource-sensitive zoning and planning that complements the park. Help communities to see the economic benefits associated with protecting nonfederal sections of a significant area.

•**Know the arguments and strategies of opponents of NPS land acquisition.** Anticipate their involvement in land-acquisition issues at your park, and be prepared to counter them.

Chapter 8

Managing Visitor Impact

I frequently tramped eight or ten miles through the deepest snow to keep an appointment with a beech tree, or a yellow birch, or an old acquaintance among the pines.

Henry David Thoreau

MANAGING VISITOR IMPACT

Americans love to visit their parks. In 1980, the last year the Park Service comprehensively studied the impact of visitors on parks, the number of visits to national parks was tallied at 210 million. In 1992, that number climbed to more than 274 million visits. (See the chart on page 104.) Experts predict that by the year 2010, nearly half a billion people will visit the park system annually. This popularity is not without a price.

Recently, the National Park Service was forced to hire a new full-time employee for the Statue of Liberty National Monument in New York. His job? To scrape off the more than 600 pounds of chewing gum left by visitors on Ellis Island's benches, railings and walls. Rangers at Canyonlands National Park, as well as at other parks in the Southwest, have reported finding centuries-old Native American pictographs and petroglyphs defaced by spray paint and sacred, ancient gravesites looted by vandals. Similar acts have been reported at Eastern parks containing the burial sites of soldiers from the colonial and Civil wars.

At Great Smoky Mountains National Park in Tennessee, where visitors drove 3.6 million vehicles through in 1992 alone, auto emissions have caused a decline in visibility, from 30 miles in the 1960s to 15 miles today, and have seriously harmed roughly 70 native plant species within the park. During peak summer vacation months, rangers at Maine's Acadia National Park have been forced to issue health warnings at the park's entrance stations about the hazardous ozone levels created by the exhaust fumes from visitors' cars.

Whether the effect is vandalism or pollution from overuse, the cause is clear. Increased visitation threatens both park resources and visitor enjoyment. The rising tide of park visitation has been accompanied by the same ills associated with increased population density anywhere—congestion, resource degradation and conflict. The survival of sensitive resources such as delicate vegetation, endangered wildlife, and rare historical and cultural artifacts becomes more precarious as more people visit the park system and use it for a wider range of recreational activities.

Visitors interfering with the enjoyment of other visitors is also a growing problem as the demands of people with different recreational interests collide. In particular, park users have clashed over motorized and nonmotorized forms of recreation (such as off-road-vehicle use vs. hiking). In the recent past, conflicts have arisen between canoeists and motorboaters at Voyageurs National Park in Minnesota, as well as between cross-country skiers and snowmobilers at Grand Teton National Park in Wyoming.

Although foreigners continue to visit American parks in growing numbers, most parks are ill-equipped to alert non-English-speaking visitors that the areas they are visiting are environmentally sensitive. During peak season at some parks, foreign tourists constitute the majority of park users. Studies at Death Valley have found that more than 70 percent of its summer visitors are foreign. Still, almost all signs found at national parks are in English, even though for a growing number of Americans it is either a second language or is not spoken at all.

The "graying of America" and people's changing vacation habits will create new visitor management challenges. The use of backcountry trails and campgrounds has declined by as much as 50 percent in some parks since the peak year of 1978. That decline means a greater percentage of park visitors are concentrated along narrow road corridors and at visitor facilities. Since senior citizens have greater flexibility in their schedules, they are largely responsible for the surge of visitation during the off-peak or "shoulder" months in spring and fall.

In many parks, it is not the visitors but their cars that are creating the problems. It is estimated that 95 percent of park visitors arrive by private vehicle. Overuse of cars has not only brought environmental threats to parks, including ozone levels which damage sensitive trees and plant life; it has also strained a road system designed for the modest visitation levels of 50 years ago. If visitation continues to rise at the current rate and maintenance continues to be deferred, the cost of repairs necessary to bring roads within the park system up to federal standards may reach $2 billion by the end of the century. It could cost taxpayers a projected $300 million to repair the road system within Yellowstone National Park alone.

Visitor management plans are of growing importance to parks as the number of visitors rises. By law, the National Park Service is now required to establish visitor "carrying capacities" when drafting a general management plan for a park. Carrying capacity is a measure of the number of visitors a park can sustain without damage to its natural resources or the quality of visitor enjoyment.

When a visitor management plan is being developed for a park, groups that are affected, such as particular recreation groups, can always be counted on to defend their interests. It is important that you, as a park advocate, take an active interest in the management of visitors to your park to ensure that the integrity of its natural resources is as securely protected as visitors' continued recreational enjoyment.

Defining Recreational Carrying Capacity

During the early decades of the park system, the National Park Service actively promoted the parks as vacation destinations. At that time, most of the parks were remote and struggling to prove their value to American society. By the 1950s, however, modern transportation and the changing demographics of the American population meant that even the most distant parks were within a day's drive of major population centers.

After World War II, parks saw a sharp increase in visitation. Within the next three decades, this boom brought calls for the parks to limit visitors. In 1978, Congress responded to the concern by requiring that the National Park Service establish "carrying capacities" when drafting general management plans.

Subsequent management policies issued by NPS have directed that parks must ensure that all recreational uses and activities within their boundaries "are not carried out in derogation of the values and purposes for which the park was established." To this end, parks are required to address visitor-impact issues and to establish specific carrying capacities in activity-specific plans (such as ones regulating river use, off-road-vehicle use or wilderness management) or in the drafting of their general management plans.

Visitors at National Parks by Year
(in millions)*

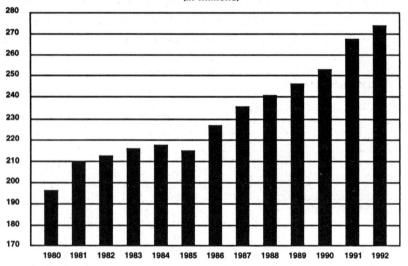

*Based on latest figures from the National Park Service

Unfortunately, Congress did not specify how it wanted visitor carrying capacities determined. In 1982, the National Parks and Conservation Association, realizing the lack of criteria for determining how many visitors a park could sustain without damaging its resources, began to develop a method for evaluating carrying capacity.

Working with scientists, NPCA reviewed the mass of research literature available on recreational impacts on soils, vegetation, wildlife, water, and the visitor experience. It then summed up its findings in a report entitled *Visitor Impact Man-*

agement: A Review of Research.

The main conclusion reached by NPCA and other recreation researchers was that no single optimum number of visitors can be defined for a park. There are too many variables involved with both the resources and the visitors. Instead, planners should try to find the level of visitation at which both the park's natural resources are protected and the visitors' experience is maintained.

Five major principles should be kept in mind when a park is developing a plan for managing visitor impact:

•**An activity's impact may be complex**. The impact of a recreational activity on an environment will never be predictable or clear-cut. It will depend on the type of activity, the number of participants involved and the season, among other factors. Some forms of impact are more obvious than others (as when off-trail hiking results in trampled vegetation), but more often than not, careful observation of a combination of indicators will be necessary to determine what effects a recreational activity has had on your park's wildlife or natural resources, if any.

•**Impact may be caused by 100 participants or by one**. A greater number of participants in an activity does not necessarily result in greater ecological damage. Most impacts do not have a direct linear relationship with number of visitors. In fact, studies have found that the greatest amount of impact occurs with initial use.

•**Not all visitor activity is harmful**. Not all wildlife or natural resources respond in the same way to visitor activity. While a recreational activity may cause a sensitive species to decline, another species may not be harmed in any way by it or may even benefit from increased human activity.

•**Every activity will have a different impact**. Some recreational activities cause greater, and more immediate, impact than others. For example, horseback riders frequently cause more erosion on trails than hikers. Even the impact caused by a given activity may vary according to the type of equipment used and the number and behavior of the participants.

•**"When" and "where" affect impact**. An activity's impact will likely depend on a variety of seasonal and site-specific variables. For example, many bird species are more sensitive to human activity during breeding and nesting season than at other times of the year.

The Visitor Impact Management Process

The following Visitor Impact Management process is a step-by-step guide to assist park planners in assessing what effect visitors' activities would have and how they should best be managed. It provides a logical approach for planners to use in identifying an activity's potential impact and formulating strategies to prevent damage to the park's resources.

•Step 1: Gather Baseline Information.

Gather all the preexisting information relevant to the situation. This should include not only information on the affected resources but also on the management policies and legal mandates in effect for the area. Policy plans (agency-wide and local), visitation records, visitor surveys and previous resource studies can all be useful sources of data.

During this review, you should clearly define the physical area that is being assessed. This might simply be a trailhead, a campground or a scenic overlook. Or you might focus on a specific resource, such as the habitat for an endangered species or an archaeological ruin. During a review for the general management plan, you'll want to look at the park as a whole.

•Step 2: Choose Your Objective.

Perhaps the most important step in achieving acceptable visitor impact is to set clearly defined objectives for an area. In other words, define the condition of the resource and the quality of the visitor experience you wish to maintain.

Traditionally, park managers have been reluctant to make decisions that may favor one type of recreational activity over another. While it may be an unpleasant task, the decision will be made by default if it's not done deliberately. This is where your involvement is crucial. Public opinion can greatly influence the development of park management objectives.

•Step 3: Choose an Indicator to Measure Impact.

This step involves identifying measurable indicators or attributes for the objectives outlined in the previous step; in other words, define how the specified conditions and experiences will be measured. The best indicators are those which are directly observable, easy to measure, sensitive to changing conditions and manageable.

•Step 4: Identify the Standards You Wish to Maintain.

The environmental conditions and the quality of recreational experience that you wish to maintain should be formulated in measurable units, such as preserving the width of a trail or limiting the number of encounters a canoeist or fisherman may have with other groups on a river. This step, in essence, is the quantification of your management objectives. You'll measure the information you gather against these standards.

•Step 5: Gather Data on Current Conditions.

Observe the current conditions and compare them to the ideal standards you wish to maintain. You'll need to measure and record the data at regular intervals. Use checklists to record your observations. Many parks will have checklists already to evaluate the condition of their campgrounds, including such measurements as the amount of bare ground, and the number and size of fire rings and campsites.

If the current conditions meet or exceed the standards established in Step 4, then you only need to monitor the situation for future changes. If the site doesn't measure up to the standards, then you need to determine the causes of impact and develop management strategies for dealing with them.

•Step 6: Identify the Probable Cause of Impact.

To find a strategy to deal with an impact problem, you must first identify the cause. Pollution at a lake may be caused by wildlife activity, not human recreation. A trail's width may be excessively wide not because of the number of users, but because it is open too early in wet springs when it is prone to be muddy, thus forcing visitors to walk along the edges.

In examining the cause of impact, it is important to review all the aspects of visitor use, such as the length of visitors' stays, the size of groups, their behavior and the frequency of periods of high use of the park.

Profile: Bob Hansen

On a busy summer day, Yosemite National Park sees 25,000 tourists—many of them experiencing the natural grandeur of the place through the windows of tour buses and air-conditioned cars which roll into the Visitors Center parking lot and leave by sunset. But if there is one small silver lining to all of the problems the traffic brings to the park, it's located slightly above the rear bumper on many of those cars—in the form of a Yosemite license plate sold through the Yosemite Fund.

Forty-five-year-old Bob Hansen lived in and worked at Yosemite for six years before becoming the Fund's executive director in 1990. Where he once taught outdoor education to kids standing amongst the giant sequoias in Yosemite's Merced Grove, he's now settled down into the more urban confines of the Fund's downtown San Francisco office, where he oversees an ambitious fundraising program that includes everything from old-fashioned grassroots begging to marketing license plates and checkbook designs.

The Yosemite license plate is one of a growing number of entrepreneurial ways some park support groups have devised to help cushion the blow of visitor impact on the national parks and, in the process, help fund them. With visitor impact—especially in popular destinations like Yosemite—on the rise, parks are also looking to tap more sophisticated private-support methods to realize even the most basic goals outlined in their general management plans.

The Yosemite Fund solicits donations—and funnels revenues from sales of items like the license plates—to support a broad range of park projects that have awaited funding since the Yosemite General Management Plan was drawn up in 1980. Thanks largely to the Fund, park managers have begun reintroducing bighorn sheep and peregrine falcons into their natural habitats, restoring wilderness areas and trails, conducting needed wildlife surveys, and have started a number of other programs. Since 1985, the Fund has raised over $3.5 million for such park improvements culled from over 35,000 donors—from corporate executives to altruistic kids with spare rolls of pennies.

Hansen uses what he calls a "venture-capital" approach to fundraising, tapping a wide variety of sources and entering business partnerships which ultimately benefit the Fund. The Fund works with the Department of Motor Vehicles to help sell its license plate program and with Bank of America in selling personal checkbook designs.

But with cars posing a mounting environmental threat to Yosemite, does Hansen see license plate sales as sending a mixed signal to the public? "We see it the other way around," he says. "The license plate is a way for people to show their concern for Yosemite every day, everywhere they go. It's not an advertisement as much as it is a message that Yosemite needs help—from everyone." The 10,000 license plate sales in the first year, he notes, raised $17,000 for the park. Of each first-year $50 license plate fee, $17 goes directly to the Yosemite Fund.

Hansen admits that, compared to most other national parks, Yosemite isn't a hard sell for those willing to give. Still, he argues that the multi-task fundraising model he's implemented at the Yosemite Fund can serve any underfunded park. "No matter what kind of park, there's a mix of fundraising opportunities that in some formula will work. It doesn't matter who the client is."

In addition to marketing a variety of products, revenue from which flows into the park's improvement projects, the Yosemite Fund solicits corporate and foundation grants, and is now focusing more actively on memorial and estate contributions, a source Hansen feels has gone untapped for too long.

"Many national parks have a special lifetime importance to people," Hansen says, recalling that it is the giant sequoias that will always draw him back to Yosemite several times a year. "Those people that have that kind of connection are prospects for a memorial contribution at the end of their lives or a planned gift during the course of their lives—and it doesn't make any difference what or where the park is. It might be Yosemite, a Civil War battlefield, a statue or Pearl Harbor. People have these heart connections to a park and that translates into a tremendous amount of philanthropy. That's a big opportunity for the parks that hasn't been developed."

•Step 7: Identify Management Strategies.

Once the probable cause of impact is understood, you can begin to devise management strategies to fix the situation. The chart on page 111 shows some potential strategies for controlling visitor impact. Direct approaches are geared toward regulating visitors' recreational activities, while indirect approaches seek to influence visitors' behavior.

Management techniques aimed at reducing a particular impact problem may create additional concerns. For example, installing a portable toilet at a trailhead that has a problem with human waste may be an attractive option, but it may be costly to service or compromise the wilderness nature of the area.

•Step 8: Implement a Management Strategy.

A management strategy must be implemented as soon as possible to prevent an increase in impacts. Strategies should not be set in stone, though, and should remain flexible as conditions change. Once a management program has been implemented, make sure the park establishes a monitoring program to regularly assess the effectiveness of the strategies and to determine whether there are any unwanted side effects.

The Car Crisis

On a busy weekend during peak season, gridlock can make some park entrances look like traffic jams. Instead of looking at a park's magnificent scenery, many visitors spend most of their time searching for a parking space. A recent study of Great Smoky Mountains National Park showed visitors spend seven times as much time inside their vehicles as outside of them—and 16 percent of the park's visitors never even leave their cars.

The answer is not necessarily to build more roads and bigger parking lots. Almost 33 percent of the 4,860 miles of paved roads in the national park system have been deemed in "poor or failed condition" by the Federal Highway Administration. Consequently, most of the funding available for roads is devoted to fixing them, not to building new ones. Furthermore, when asphalt is added to a park, the natural resources are usually the losers.

About 40 national parks have successfully instituted some form of mass transit as an alternative to car use, including

Visitor Management Strategies

INDIRECT

Physical Alterations
- Improve or neglect access
- Improve or neglect campsites
- Make trails more or less difficult

Information Dispersal
- Advertise area attributes
- Identify other visitation opportunities
- Provide minimal impact education
- Advertise current use levels

Eligibility Constraints
- Charge constant fees
- Charge differential fees
- Require proof of skills

(Adapted from *Wilderness Management*, second edition revised, John C. Hendee, George H. Stankey and Robert Lucas, North American Press, Golden, Colorado, 1990.)

DIRECT

Enforcement
- Increase surveillance
- Impose fines

Zoning
- Separate incompatible users
- Limit length of stay at certain sites
- Prohibit use at certain times

Rationing Use Intensity
- Limit group size
- Limit use via access points
- Limit use via campsite
- Rotate use
- Require reservations

Restricting Activities
- Restrict type of use
- Limit length of stay
- Restrict camping practices

shuttles, light rail and ferries. Some of these systems are strictly internal. Others, usually in urban areas, are integrated into regional mass transit. Grand Canyon National Park offers both a steam train to the South Rim from nearby Williams, Arizona and a bus shuttle system that operates three different loops within the park. Ridership of the train, which began service in 1989, has averaged about 100,000 visitors a year, although it has the capacity to service 386,000 park visitors a year. Even this is just a small dent in the total number of people visiting the canyon—over 4.2 million in 1992, bringing 1.2 million cars into the park.

The most pressing challenge facing park planners is not what to do with the burgeoning numbers of park visitors, but what to do with their cars. Look for ways to keep a cap on the number of cars coming into your park. Your support of plans to reduce the number of visiting automobiles will be of vital importance to both the protection of park resources and the quality of the visitor experience.

How You Can Get Involved in Visitor Management Issues

•**Become familiar with the visitor use problems and issues at your park.** Make your own observations and discuss with park staff. Ask park staff for any information that they may have on visitor use levels and patterns. Many parks have conducted visitor use studies. At a minimum, all parks prepare visitor activity reports that are submitted to the regional office. Find out if the park has ever conducted a survey of its visitor-impact problems.

•**Determine if legal requirements to set visitor carrying capacities are being met.** If your park is developing a general management plan, ask park staff how it will meet the requirements to set visitor carrying capacities. Participate in any scoping opportunities (see Chapter 11, "Planning for Parks") and encourage park planners to manage visitor impact.

•**If traffic is a problem, see if mass transit alternatives have ever been studied.** If alternatives haven't been explored, ask your U.S. representative to request funding for a study.

•**See if park visitor information includes advice on minimizing impacts.** There are various sources of visitor information available at your park (visitor center exhibits, brochures, overlook signs, trail literature). Evaluate them to see if they include suggestions on how visitors can reduce their effect on park resources. Make suggestions to park staff on how they can improve or expand such messages.

Chapter 9

Protecting Park Water Resources

A wilderness...is hereby recognized as an area where the earth and its community of life are untrammeled by man, where man himself is a visitor who does not remain.

Wallace Stegner (from the Wilderness Act)

PROTECTING PARK
WATER RESOURCES

In the 1800s, the waters of the Everglades sustained an amazing abundance of biological diversity: wildlife including American crocodiles, Florida panthers and snail kite; 300 species of land birds, water birds and birds of prey; and nearly 125 kinds of fish which thrived in the rivers, creeks and estuaries of the Florida Bay. Together they formed a delicate and complex ecosystem, one that depended on the ebb and flow of floods precipitated by the region's seasonal semi-tropical monsoons.

Today that world is endangered, thanks to development which has diverted, dammed and otherwise damaged the area's waters. Over the past 100 years, the creation of a massive water management system, designed to serve the needs of South Florida's expanding population and agricultural industry, has upset the Everglades' natural hydrological flows.

Even though it was protected as a national park in 1947, and later as an International Biosphere in 1976, the region's population of wading birds has decreased 95 percent since the '30s, from 265,000 to less than 15,000 today. Other populations face extinction, among them the white ibis and nesting wood storks, as well as the native panther. Chemical and nutrient pollution from agriculture, and nearby oil exploration and drilling, have seriously harmed water quality, ravaging entire populations of fish and shrimp in the park's southern end. There are even plans to tap into precious ground water three miles from the park's border and pump 140 million gallons per day to surrounding cities, a step that could deplete water resources within the park.

Everglades National Park is just one park among many whose water resources are under siege. A recent survey by the National Park Service identified 480 significant water-related threats to more than 170 parks—nearly half of those in the entire park system. While the threats range from diversion to pollution, outside influences threaten both the quantity and quality of park waters—often from miles beyond parks' protective boundaries. Some of the threats include:

•**Proposed dams, diversions and hydropower plants upstream of park boundaries** which could dry up, diminish or radically alter park river flows. Builders of a proposed hydropower facility hope to divert 40 percent of the water from Colorado's Gunnison River that now flows through Black Canyon of the Gunnison National Monument. According to one study, this could have "adverse and irreversible" effects on the plant and animal life within the park, as well as on whitewater rafting on the river. Similarly, more than 50 dams have been proposed around Washington's Olympic National Park. Damming rivers has been proposed outside Dinosaur National Monument and Zion National Park as well.

•**Proposals to pump ground water from underground aquifers** to support urban, agricultural and industrial development also could dry up park springs and seeps by lowering local water tables. Currently, the Las Vegas Water District is seeking permission to drill 146 wells to pump water from the aquifer of Nevada's Death Valley National Monument into the homes and swimming pools of Las Vegas. Any drop in ground water levels could dry up the more than 400 desert springs that sustain the area's snails, bighorn sheep, coyotes and bobcats.

The drilling of almost 1,000 wells in the seven miles surrounding Oklahoma's Chickasaw National Recreation Area, and the pumping of more than 1.6 million gallons of water per day from its aquifer, may have sapped the park's freshwater and mineral springs: Nearly half of the springs have dried up already and scientists predict that other major springs will dry up

Chemical and nutrient runoff from agricultural development threaten the delicate ecosystem of Everglades National Park.

within the next decade.

• **Pollution from industrial, urban and agricultural activities** which threatens the safety of park waters. Threats include leaching of toxins from abandoned mines and landfills, chemical fertilizer and pesticide runoff from agricultural or residential areas, industrial discharge, urban wastewater and sewage runoff.

Over the past two decades, the wetlands comprising 25 percent of Virginia's Colonial National Historic Park have been battered by chemical, sewage and oil spills. Dangerous abandoned mine openings lace Arizona's Grand Canyon National Park, California's Joshua Tree National Monument and Alaska's Wrangell-St. Elias National Park, where rangers found petroleum distillates, lead products and lime at a number of the park's more than 400 abandoned sites. Major acid spills and toxic discharge by Canadian industries over the past 30 years have severely tainted the Columbia River flowing into Washington's Coulee Dam National Recreation Area.

• **Logging, grazing, road building and other construction activities adjacent to parks** which could alter park waters with erosion, sedimentation and pollutant runoff. Recent overcutting of timber along Washington's Skagit River, which runs through North Cascades National Park, has clogged it with silt, decreasing the fish population and increasing flooding—despite the Skagit's having been designated a Wild and Scenic River in 1978. Construction projects and agricultural development alongside the St. Croix and Lower St. Croix National Scenic Waterway in Wisconsin and Minnesota have caused steep ravines to erode and introduced sediment and heavy metal pollutants into the river. High levels of pesticides have been found in native fish.

The National Park Service has no single tool for protecting park waters. Rather, NPS and concerned citizens must rely on a complex patchwork of statutes, regulations, legal doctrines and administrative procedures. Effective use of many of these tools may often require experienced technical or legal assistance, and it is always a good idea to seek such assistance if it is available. Even without technical and legal help, however, you can help protect park waters by taking many of the actions described below.

A good resource is the National Park Service's Water Resources Division in Fort Collins, Colorado. Its mission is to provide research and training throughout the park system. The Division also takes action where feasible to aid park staffs in protecting water resources. Although you should primarily work through your local park superintendent and staff, the Water Resources Division may be able to provide needed technical, scientific or legal assistance on park water issues. The Division's address is: 1201 Oak Ridge Drive, Suite 250, Fort Collins, CO 80525.

Legal Underpinnings of Water Protection

The primary legal basis for protecting park water resources against threats to water quantity is the "reserved rights" doctrine. The doctrine was originally developed by the U.S. Supreme Court to protect Native Americans' right to the water needed for productive use on tribal reservations. The federal government's reserved rights are based on the principle that whenever the U.S. Congress withdraws or reserves land from the public domain for particular purposes, it simultaneously protects sufficient water to fulfill the purposes of that reservation.

Generally considered to cover both surface and ground waters, a reserved right protects the amount of water necessary to serve the purposes for which a park was created and no more. A park's purposes are stated in its enabling legislation or proclamation as well as by the Organic Act, which states that the "fundamental purpose" of all units of the National Park System "is to conserve the scenery and the natural and historic objects and wildlife therein and to provide for the enjoyment of the same." Thus, for most parks the amount of water protected under the reserved right should be the natural or existing water flows or levels.

In order to assert and defend reserved rights claims, the National Park Service has developed a complex process for identifying the amount of water a park needs. First, within the broad purposes for which a park has been established (the protection of natural resources), NPS identifies specific resources (such as native fish populations) whose water needs can be studied. Next, it develops scientific proof that certain volumes and timing of flows constitute the minimum amount of water needed to avoid impairment of park resources. To determine those minimum flows, the Park Service studies existing conditions related to the health of the specific resources (such as the water temperature or depth fish require at key life stages). Using computer modeling, NPS then analyzes the potential effects of reduced water flows.

The use of reserved rights to protect park waters depends on the system of water law under which a particular state operates. Each state has a distinct set of water laws, but two basic doctrines for allocation of surface waters prevail. Generally, Western states operate under the appropriative system and Eastern states under the riparian system, although some states operate under water laws that are a mixture of the two.

•The Appropriative System

In Western states, water rights are governed according to the "prior appropriation" doctrine. In the past, a person simply had to put a quantity of water to a "beneficial" use, usually an economic one such as mining, irrigation or domestic use, to obtain a water right. Today, a party is required to file an application for a water right before using water from a public source. An applicant must show that water will be put to an economically beneficial use (such as irrigation). Upon approval, water can be diverted from its source only for that purpose.

Under this system, water rights are granted based on the chronological order in which applications were filed, or in some cases, based on the order in which water was diverted or put to use. This principle is often referred to as "first in time, first in right." If a stream becomes "overappropriated," in that the water rights issued for it are in excess of the stream's actual water, then the holder of the oldest water right receives first entitlement, then the second oldest and so on down the line, until the water supply is exhausted. A national park with federal reserved rights establishes its place in line based on the date of its designation.

In most states operating under the appropriative system, the right to use water is regulated and administered by the state water engineer. The water engineer's office keeps records of water use, receives and retains approval over applications for new water uses, conducts and reviews studies of hydrologic conditions, and appoints river commissioners or water masters to supervise the distribution of water rights.

Water rights are sometimes determined under general adjudications—comprehensive proceedings designed to adjudicate all the water rights for a particular stream, river basin or region. Under this process, a state requires each party claiming a right to water from a particular stream to assert its claim and to submit evidence supporting it. The National Park Service must come forward and file claims for park water needs or else *forfeit its water rights*. In what can develop into complex and lengthy litigation, the state court then determines who has a legitimate water right and quantifies the amount of water protected under that right.

Although the National Park Service has filed claims for more than 130 park units in preparation for formal adjudication, very rarely have courts had cause to actually conduct these proceedings. In recent years, a number of cases have occurred in Colorado and Wyoming, with mixed results. In adjudicating NPS' reserved water rights for Dinosaur National Monument, the Colorado Court narrowly interpreted the amount of water reserved for the monument under its establishing proclamation to be the minuscule amount necessary to preserve the park's dinosaur bones—thus failing to protect the Green and Yampa rivers which flow through the monument and which are essential to its natural, scenic and recreational values.

States also issue water rights on an ongoing basis, usually through proceedings conducted by the state engineer. Applicants are usually required to submit a written application identifying the amount of water requested, the point of diversion and the proposed use. In most states, notice of the application must be published in local or regional newspapers. Upon application, other parties, including other water-right holders, then have the right to file a written "protest" challenging the application if they believe it will diminish the quantity of water protected by a senior water right. In most states, protests may also be filed by any party who believes the public interest could be harmed by the granting of a water right.

Given that Western states favor the "economically beneficial" use of water (and given that the short-term economic benefit of the preservation of scenic beauty is often harder to prove than that of a hydropower facility, for example), park advocates there must aggressively assert the reserved rights of national parks, if those rights are senior to a proposed action. Otherwise, the best recourse is to lodge a formal protest to a proposed diversion or damming, citing the action's threat to public interest.

The Riparian System

In most of the East and Midwest, where water supply has generally exceeded demand, water rights are allocated and disputes are resolved under the "riparian" doctrine. Under this system, every landowner bordering on a stream has a right to use a "reasonable" quantity of water as long as that use does not interfere with the "reasonable" use of water by other adjacent landowners. The order in which landowners began using water does not necessarily establish any special priority to water. If demand increases, or in times of shortage, the available water supply is shared by all water-right holders based on the principle of "reasonable use."

How the concept of reserved rights applies in the riparian system remains unclear, largely because the courts have not addressed this issue. Most parks in states operating under the riparian system lack reserved rights since they were established from purchased or donated private lands rather than through the "reservation" of public lands.

Under the riparian system, parks that border a stream, or into which a stream flows, theoretically have a right to a "reasonable use" of that water. A park's riparian right, however, is vulnerable to damaging reductions as other parties' demands on water increase, or if shortages occur. In addition, to protect park flows against damaging reduction, the National Park Service must be able to demonstrate, in litigation if necessary, that com-

How To Protect Park Water Quantity

•**Intervene in any adjudication process to help protect the park's reserved water rights.** Keep informed about the status of the park's water right and any demands on water sources that could threaten resources. Encourage the park superintendent to take whatever steps necessary to ensure that the park's water right is properly adjudicated and quantified, unless sound reasons exist for deferring or avoiding those steps.

Ask to see a copy of any claim filed for the purpose of asserting park water rights if the park is in a state operating under the appropriative system and your park was "reserved" from public lands. Check to see if the document claims water for all the purposes identified in the park's enabling act or proclamation and the Organic Act. The National Park Service is sometimes under pressure from pro-water development politicians to limit the purposes for which water is claimed.

•**Protest water-right applications for projects that could harm park waters.** Be alert for any project or activity that could diminish the flows in park streams by damming or diverting upstream flows or that could deplete park springs by pumping ground water from local aquifers. Encourage the Park Service to visit the local water engineer's office periodically and review any water-right applications filed on park watershed lands. If you have the time, you can do this yourself. The earlier you learn about such projects, the greater your opportunity to influence their future.

If you learn about a project that may threaten park waters, inform your superintendent and encourage the assistance of the National Park Service Water Resources Division. If you do this in writing, send a copy of your letter to the NPS regional office and to the NPS Water Resources Division.

Visit your local state water engineer's office and ask if a water right has been issued or water-right change application has been filed for the project. If a water right has already been issued, check its date. If it is junior to the park, you may still have an opportunity to raise concerns that the project will diminish water protected under the park's senior right. If a water-right application is pending, find out the deadline and the format for

Profile: Liane Russell

All politics, as they say, is local. If that's true, then Dr. Liane Russell—through four decades of environmental advocacy—has beaten the odds.

She was an outsider in every sense of the word when she landed a research job at Tennessee's Oak Ridge National Laboratories in 1947 at the age of 24. Born and raised in Austria, Russell had joined thousands of other European immigrants who passed through Ellis Island when she moved with her family to New York City during the Depression of the 1930s. She was later educated at the University of Chicago, then moved with her husband, William, and made a permanent home in Tennessee. Together, the two earnest and soft-spoken Northerners and the Dixie South were an odd mix.

Russell, now 71, is still doing genetic research as a biologist in Oak Ridge, and her neighbors have gotten to know her a lot better—mostly as a determined, hard-working environmental activist who has fought to protect *their* wilderness areas and rivers from dams, development and a host of other environmental threats since the 1940s.

"There was a strong feeling when we moved here that we weren't wanted. We'd be at a meeting and some local person would say, 'I want everyone who's from around here to raise their hand.'" Russell wrangles her best Appalachian drawl out of her German accent, now faint. "They were tryin' to cast *'spersions* on the *outsiduhs*."

It didn't take long for Russell to settle in. Russell, who had hiked in the Austrian Alps as a child, had been even more awestruck with a uniquely American wonder—wilderness—that surrounded the Tennessee greenbelt and its whitewater rivers. In 1966, she and her husband William joined a dozen or so willing neighbors and founded the Tennessee Citizens for Wilderness Planning (TCWP), a formidable wilderness-protection group which now numbers more than 500.

Her first battle was to stop a power line from running through the local greenbelt. Since then, Russell has led the group's efforts to fight dam construction on the Big South Fork, and to ensure the river's protection by its inclusion in the National Park system. Next on the list was the Obed River and its tributaries, which run through Tennessee's Cumberland Mountains, carving out dramatic 500-foot gorges, and offering the most challenging whitewater and pristine wilderness areas in the eastern United States.

"When we first started talking about protecting the Obed," Russell says, "one of the local politicians said, 'It's nothin' but a dirty crack in the ground full of rattlesnakes.'" Two years after the designation of the Big South Fork National River and Recreation Area, the other "crack in the ground" in Tennessee, the Obed, became an official Wild and Scenic River. More recently, Russell and the TCWP have been fighting construction of a proposed dam on an Obed tributary. "After seeing something like the Obed, I couldn't stand the thought of see-

ing it covered in 400 feet of water," she says.

In 1993, the National Parks and Conservation Association honored Russell for her 25 years of work in park protection, giving her its highest citizen's award for efforts on behalf of national parks. Still, the earnest Dr. Russell is taken aback by the suggestion that she's done anything extraordinary. "Many of those who have lived here as long as we have still haven't seen what a treasure they have here. If they did, they might be doing the same thing."

filing a protest. Be aware that you can request and receive deadline extensions.

Encourage the park superintendent to seek assistance from the National Park Service's Water Resources Division in filing a protest challenging any application for a water right that could diminish park waters. Ask for a copy of the protest and use it as a model to file your own protest. A protest can consist simply of a letter stating your objection to issuance of the water right because of potential adverse impact on park waters. Demand that the water-right application be denied unless the applicant demonstrates that the proposed water use will not harm park waters.

Outstanding Natural Resource Waters

A little-used Environmental Protection Agency regulation under the Clean Water Act provides the best tool for protecting the quality of park waters. The provision designates "high quality" waters, including National Park System waters, as Outstanding National Resource Waters (ONRW) and establishes a nondegradation standard for their protection.

The ONRW designation is the most rigorous of several water-quality standards adopted by EPA to avoid further degradation of existing water quality. EPA has explained that "high quality" waters include waters of pristine quality, and waters that are "important, unique or sensitive ecologically, but whose quality as measured by traditional parameters may not be particularly high or whose character cannot be adequately described by these parameters." This means that park waters such as swamps and hot springs, which might not be considered high quality under traditional standards, can be protected under the designation.

As defined in the regulations, the ONRW designation and standard provide a significant tool for protecting park waters from the individual and cumulative impacts of activities upstream and beyond park boundaries. Furthermore, because recent case law requires upstream states to avoid violation of the anti-degradation standards of downstream states, ONRW designation could also offer protection to park waters from activities beyond state borders.

Unfortunately, EPA has not treated its ONRW regulation as mandatory. As a result, many states have failed to designate park waters as ONRWs. Some states have created designations with similar titles but weaker standards. For example, some states allow degradation of "high quality" waters if there are significant "economic" benefits. In contrast, EPA's regulation imposes an essentially unqualified nondegradation standard.

Important opportunities exist, however, for you to help shape your state's water-quality standards and to establish protective designations for park waters.

Under the Clean Water Act, each state is required to designate all its surface waters for a particular use or combination of uses. States may propose changes in their designated uses at any time. However, the act requires them to review their standards every three years and, if necessary, to revise their designated uses according to the rules laid down in EPA's regulations. This mandatory triennial process affords the opportunity for you to seek ONRW or similar designations for park waters and to urge that the standards protecting these waters be strengthened if necessary. The National Park Service has the same opportunity and should be encouraged to take advantage of it.

How To Protect Park Water Quality

•**Ensure that the important role of park waters is fully recognized in park planning documents.** Review your park's general management plan and statement for management. If these plans do not describe the importance of park waters, the existing and potential threats to park waters, and the measures needed to assure their protection, request that they be amended. Urge your superintendent to initiate such a plan, if your park does not have a water resources management plan.

•**Review existing park programs and urge improvements** to ensure that the necessary data to defend park waters is being developed. Ask the park superintendent or natural resource specialists what programs are under way to inventory and monitor park waters, to identify and investigate existing and potential pollution problems, and to identify and quantify water needs. Urge the superintendent to establish such programs if they do not exist. Pass your recommendations on to the director of the appropriate National Park Service regional office. If NPS says funding is a problem, write to your state's U.S. senators and representatives and urge that they seek funding for the needed water resource programs.

• **Seek designation of park water resources as Outstanding National Resource Waters** or whatever similar designation your state may have established. Similarly, urge your state to adopt strong standards that protect designated park waters from degradation.

Learn about the special designations and standards available. Find out the process for recommending revisions in such designations and standards by calling your state's environmental quality or natural resources division. Some states will have clearly delineated criteria that a water body must meet to be designated; others will not. If your state has not already developed procedures, it is possible to influence how it goes about structuring and defining its application process. Investigate and learn the existing category of water-quality standards that the state has applied to any waters of significance in your park. If the standards applied are unacceptably weak, find out why an ONRW or other higher standard has not been applied.

Develop information on the location, quality and value of park waters. Confer with park staff and seek their involvement and assistance in this effort. Encourage the Park Service to initiate programs to inventory and monitor park water quality if such programs do not already exist. Urge the Park Service to petition the state for special designation and strict protection of park waters. You can call or write the NPS Water Resource Division to seek assistance or support for your efforts.

Chapter 10

Protecting Park Air Quality

There is no need for wilderness or species preservation to hinder economic growth, or for economic growth to prevent such preservation. On all dimensions, preservation represents a gift to the future.

Lester C. Thurow

10

PROTECTING PARK AIR QUALITY

There may be no view in America more indelible than that of the Grand Canyon—but on many days it can't be seen by visitors, obscured as it is by a thick haze.

The source of the pollution? A 1987 Park Service study found that some of the emissions originated as far away as Los Angeles, but others could be traced to the Navajo Generating Station in Arizona, 80 miles northeast of the canyon. The coal-fired power plant spewed plumes of sulfur dioxide into the air daily (at a rate of 13 tons per hour) until the actions of park advocates like Christine Shaver prompted the Environmental Protection Agency to enforce the federal Clean Air Act of 1977. As a result, plant management recently installed new air pollution control measures. (See the profile of Christine Shaver on page 136.)

This is a significant victory, but it is one which demonstrates the complexities and frustrations of trying to ensure standards of air quality in our parks. Although 70 national parks and wilderness areas face serious threats from air pollution, the Grand Canyon case was the first instance since its passage in which EPA sought to enforce the park visibility protections of the Clean Air Act, and it did so only after NPCA and the Environmental Defense Fund won a lawsuit forcing the government to create a plan to improve the park's visibility.

Many national parks were established to protect their magnificent views, but these vistas are often shrouded in a haze of air pollution from a wide variety of sources. In fact, the National Park Service found in 1988 that scenic park vistas are affected by man-made haze more than 90 percent of the time. Studies have found that, over the past 40 years, sulfur dioxide from power plant emissions has caused a 50 percent decline in visibility in parks across the rural eastern United States.

Air pollution poses a dire threat not only to the natural beauty but to the health of parks as well. High levels of ozone, caused by industrial and automobile emissions, have created the need for health warnings to be posted for visitors to Maine's Acadia National Park, Virginia's Shenandoah National Park and California's Sequoia National Park. Another by-product of automobiles, nitrogen dioxide, along with sulfur dioxide, contributes to the formation of acid rain. Levels of acidity known to damage fish and vegetation have been found at Acadia, Shenandoah, Tennessee's Great Smoky Mountains National Park, Delaware Gap National Recreation Area, Colorado's Rocky Mountain National Park and Indiana Dunes National Lakeshore.

While federal legislation has given government the tools to demand that industries maintain strict air pollution controls, these laws have been enforced only too rarely. As a park advocate, you can make a difference by knowing the existing and potential threats to your park's air quality, drawing attention to them in the community at large and urging federal, state and local government to do their parts in enforcing the legislation.

The Clean Air Act

The Clean Air Act sets forth national standards for air quality that individual states must meet. It requires the development of a state implementation plan designed to meet those standards set forth in the Act, which the Environmental Protection Agency then reviews. In most cases where pollution control is necessary, provisions set by states can and should be more stringent than those required, but legally states only need to meet the Act's minimum standards. During the development of an implementation plan, a state must notify the public it is doing so and solicit public comment on the plan.

The Clean Air Act contains two overall standards of air quality which all air in the United States, including the air above national parks, should meet. The primary standards are designed to protect human health, while the secondary ones are designed to protect the public from the adverse impacts of air pollution, including its impacts on soil, water, crops, vegetation, animals, visibility and synthetic materials.

During the 1970s, it became clear that these standards were still not adequate to protect the national park resources. In the Clean Air Act Amendments of 1977, Congress enacted the Prevention of Significant Deterioration of Air Quality Program (PSD), which was designed to limit the amount of additional air pollution affecting national parks and wilderness areas located in clean-air areas and to prevent further deterioration of their air quality. The 1977 Amendments also established a program to improve visibility in a limited number of large natural parks and wilderness areas.

The Prevention of Significant Deterioration of Air Quality provisions divide parks into three different "classes" to define the levels of protection for existing air quality. Class I areas (national parks larger than 6,000 acres and international parks and national memorial parks larger than 5,000 acres in existence in 1977) receive the highest degree of protection. Other parks, including new parks added to the system after 1977, are Class II areas. States have authority, in some circumstances, to designate parks as Class III areas.

The Prevention of Significant Deterioration permitting process is designed to stop additional harmful air pollution from affecting the parks by requiring special permitting considerations before construction of a new source near a national park in a clean-air area. The EPA has interpreted "near a park" to mean within 100 kilometers (or 62 miles) of the park boundary. Sources further from the park may be required to have a PSD permit if they are very large or directly upwind from the park. A "clean-air area" is one whose air quality meets or exceeds the Clean Air Act's standards. Only specified increases over "baseline concentrations" of pollutants, or the levels of pollutants existing in the air at the time the permit request is filed, are allowed.

The PSD permitting process is triggered when a permit is requested. The baseline concentrations of pollutants are then determined. If the proposed facility may affect a Class I park, the Department of the Interior and the National Park Service must be notified.

If the National Park Service determines that the proposed source will have an adverse impact and the state agrees, the permit cannot be approved. If NPS determines there may be adverse impacts, the permit may not be issued unless the applicants demonstrate that the allowable increments will not be exceeded. If NPS certifies that there will not be adverse impacts from the proposed source, the state may issue the permit even if the increments are exceeded by a small amount.

The Difficulty of Determining Adverse Impact

Enforcement of the Prevention of Significant Deterioration provisions has been difficult, in part because, in most cases, park advocates have been hard pressed to prove that emissions from a source *single-handedly* will lead to an adverse impact on a park's air quality. Often, adverse impact is caused by the confluence of several sources. Since air quality regulations operate on a state-by-state basis, states can issue permits for potentially harmful development within their borders, arguing that the actual sources responsible for air pollution are situated in neighboring states.

Still, by bringing attention to and challenging potentially harmful development, sometimes park advocates can win concessions that can reduce threats to air quality. This was the case in September of 1990, when the National Park Service used the Prevention of Significant Deterioration process to challenge the permitting of the Multitrade coal- and waste-wood-burning power plant, proposed in Pittsylvania County, Virginia, approximately 68 miles from Shenandoah National Park.

As originally proposed, the facility would have affected Shenandoah National Park's aquatic life and vegetation, which were already impaired by air pollution. Issuing a Preliminary Determination of Adverse Impact, the first step in the PSD process, the National Park Service argued that Multitrade's emissions of nitrogen oxides, sulphur dioxide and volatile organic compounds would worsen the park's air quality, reduce visibility and subject it to even higher levels of ozone and acid rain. At the time it was proposed, Multitrade was just one of 15 new power plants slated for the state of Virginia.

Despite lobbying by the NPCA and other national and local groups in support of the National Park Service's opposition to the permit, the state air board approved the Multitrade permit. Even though the state agreed that the park's resources were being adversely affected under present conditions, it found that opponents to the permit had not shown that the proposed facility would have any additional impact on the park. The state also argued that most of the problems with the park's air quality came from sources outside Virginia.

NPCA and other groups represented by the Southern Environmental Law Center appealed the permit to EPA. The National Park Service also decided to appeal. Park advocates conducted extensive meetings with state government officials, including the governor and secretary of resources, and with Department of the Interior officials. A media campaign brought the issue to the public's attention.

The pressure paid off. Multitrade decided to negotiate with the National Park Service and the conservation groups, and eventually, in exchange for the groups' withdrawing their appeals to the EPA, Multitrade made significant concessions, including:

- agreeing not to burn coal at the facility and to operate it as a 100-percent wood-fueled power plant;
- agreeing to lower air emissions below the level the state would have permitted;
- acquiring offsets from another facility (Multitrade bought a plant and closed it down, thus lowering the total emissions entering the park);
- agreeing to make a $25,000 charitable contribution per year to promote environmental benefits (with $5,000 earmarked for Shenandoah National Park);
- agreeing to make a $25,000 contribution for studies

Profile: Christine Shaver

In the late 1980s, scientists from the National Park Service were poring over scientific data, trying to pinpoint the sources of air pollution in the Grand Canyon. The numbers pointed in part to a coal-fired power plant called the Navajo Generating Station, 80 miles away.

That put lawyer Christine Shaver, then the National Park Service's chief employee in charge of protecting the national parks from air pollution, in an unusual bind. "The Clean Air Act requirements for protecting visibility in national parks had never been used to force a cleanup," she explains. "The plant was owned by several utility companies, which had a lot of political and economic power." To make matters worse, the plant was owned in part by the same Department of Interior that ran the Park Service. It was a Catch-22.

Shaver, a former EPA lawyer who'd worked on the Clean Air Act amendments, was determined to enforce a cleanup in spite of the political obstacles. She was a lawyer with an innate sense of appreciation for the natural world. While she'd spent childhood summers touring the national parks in a camper with her family, back home in Cleveland parts of Lake Erie were restricted because of pollution and even the Cuyahoga River, which runs through Cleveland, occasionally caught fire for the same reason.

"As I was growing up, I had no idea how to clean up the pollution problems we had created or how to prevent further problems," she says. "When I joined EPA, I suddenly came upon a whole group of people who were dedicated to making things better and had the tools to do it."

After six years with EPA, Shaver joined the National Park Service as the chief of the Policy Planning and Permit Review Branch of its Air Quality Division. It was during the transition between the Reagan and Bush administrations in 1988—when the political resistance wasn't looking—that Shaver quietly began helping two outside organizations—the Environmental Defense Fund and the Grand Canyon Trust—lead the battle for compliance. She quietly fed them all the scientific data and Park Service records they needed to build an argument in court. Those organizations, in turn, turned the information over to the press.

"I made sure the issue didn't just die just because the administration didn't want to deal with it. People on the outside are more in a position to keep the heat on."

Months of negotiations followed between the power plant and environmental groups. In the end, the plant agreed to the most stringent air quality standards—a 90 percent reduction in sulfur dioxide emissions. Shaver's stealth helped push through an unprecedented victory for air quality in national parks.

"It was the first time that the Clean Air Act provisions requiring that visibility be protected in national parks had been tested," she recalls from her new office at the Environmental Defense Fund in Denver, where she now continues to work on air quality management at different sites around the U.S., and now along the border in Mexico. "It was a wonderful decision that said if a source contributed just a small portion of visibility problems in a national park, it was required to comply with the stringent controls."

After 17 years of government work, Shaver now prefers to fight environmental battles from the other side of the regulatory fence at EDF. Her work with the National Park Service, she says, "gave me a taste of how fun it is to cut a deal and make a difference, but the ability to do that at EDF is much greater than it is at EPA or the Park Service. I have much better access to high-level folks without going through the chain."

Still, the 41-year-old Shaver understands that grassroots activism is an indispensable resource in protecting the environment. "Having people put forth policies that request the highest degree of protection and fastest action really is a benefit to government agencies who are, on the other hand, hearing from affected industries that they should take their time and not worry about it," Shaver says. "In order to do their job—which is, hopefully, to protect the national parks—they need to have that pull on the other side."

Despite her impressive legal successes, Shaver considers her two daughters—10-year-old Courtney and seven-year-old Jessica—her most important contribution to environmental protection. "They don't take clean air and water for granted," she says. "They respect the rights of nature. Most important, they know that the little things they can do make a difference."

relating to nitrogen oxide emissions;
- and agreeing to support regulations requiring energy conservation efficiency and a cap on nitrogen oxide emissions for the state.

As a result, the Multitrade facility will be much less harmful to Shenandoah National Park and the environment than if it had been constructed and operated as originally planned. The compromise serves as a powerful example of both the limitations of the Prevention of Significant Deterioration permitting program and the ways in which it can be used as a framework for bringing political pressure to bear on potentially harmful development.

The Visibility Program

The 1977 amendments to the Clean Air Act also contain provisions designed to improve visibility in Class I parks. The visibility section is potentially an important tool because it can be used to require existing sources to clean up their air-polluting facilities. (These provisions were used in compelling the Navajo Generating Station in Page, Arizona to install new air pollution measures.)

EPA divided the visibility program into two phases. First, EPA required the states to control large, individual sources that were found to be degrading visibility in Class I areas. Under EPA regulations, states should require these sources to install best available retrofit technology (BART). In determining what should be considered BART for each individual plant, states may consider the cost of compliance, the energy and other environmental impacts of compliance, any existing pollution-control technology in use at the source, the remaining useful life of the plant, and the degree of improved visibility that may result from any given technology.

In the first phase, states also were required to make progress toward the long-term visibility goal: the prevention of any future and the remedying of any existing impairment of visibility in Class I areas. Under this program, even new sources in nonattainment areas could be controlled. Other steps that a state could consider are emission reductions through ongoing pollution-control programs, measures to mitigate construction impacts, better fire management and the phasing out of pollution sources. The visibility SIP is to be reevaluated every three years by the state and the National Park Service.

Under the second phase of the visibility regulations, EPA is supposed to regulate regional haze, a form of pollution from a variety of sources, often in urban areas, which combine to cause poor visibility in parks. EPA has never proposed these regulations, however. Park air quality will never be improved to the point contemplated by the Clean Air Act without regional haze regulation and implementation. The development of these regulations is on conservationists' agenda.

How to Protect Park Air Quality and Visibility

The Clean Air Act is a complex law that even the most thoughtful and dedicated park advocate may not fully comprehend. In addition to the programs specifically established by Congress to prevent significant deterioration of air quality and address visibility degradation in parks, numerous other requirements in the Clean Air Act might apply to sources of air pollution affecting parks. These requirements (such as emission limits or control requirements for existing pollution sources) should be spelled out in SIPs and/or permits and can be enforced by citizens as well as government agencies. You may need to enlist both scientific and legal expert assistance to achieve a successful resolution of air quality issues; however, you can take a number of actions on your own to scope out problems and lay foundations for solutions.

•**Build coalitions.** Developing a strong show of support for protection of park resources is critical in any dispute over park air quality.

•**Familiarize yourself with your state's implementation plan.** Each state develops its own regulations to implement the requirements of the Clean Air Act. The Act specifies the goals to be achieved, but the individual states are responsible for creating a plan that will achieve those goals.

•**Let the state know of your interest.** It is important to notify the state air-quality office that you are concerned about the air quality in your national park. The state should have a process for alerting concerned individuals that a construction or operating permit has been requested that may affect the park's air quality.

Request notification of revisions to your state's implementation plan. The Clean Air Act requires that the SIP be reassessed on a regular basis. The regulations state that the visibility SIP should be re-examined every three years. You should request notice of any proceedings by the state to amend the state implementation plan.

Ask questions. A variety of methods, vehicles, and opportunities may be available for documenting, remedying, and preventing air-pollution problems in parks. Find the right people and ask the relevant questions.

•**Notify the park staff of your interest in park air quality.** Contact park staff, in particular the resource management specialist, and ask to be put on the park's mailing list. According to EPA regulations, the National Park Service must be advised of permit requests for major sources within 100 kilometers (62 miles) of the park in some circumstances. Close coordination with the park staff will give you another opportunity to hear of pending permit requests.

You will often have to rely on Park Service science to demonstrate the harm that may be caused by a potential new source and to enforce the Clean Air Act; therefore, it is important to develop a close working relationship with park managers on air-quality issues.

•**Encourage the state's PSD efforts.** Most states have authority to administer the PSD program, and their regulations must be consistent with federal guidelines. In several areas, the state could be more aggressive in protecting park values from air pollution impacts than federal regulations require. For example, a state may redesignate lands to a higher class to give them greater protection. States may also adopt a baseline of pollution levels for parks so that any additional pollution created by a proposed facility can be better evaluated.

Chapter 11

Planning for Parks

Unless we are to betray our heritage consciously, we must make an all-out effort now to acquire the public lands which present and future generations need. Only prompt action will save prime park, forest and shoreline and other recreation lands before they are pre-empted for other purposes or priced beyond the public purse.

Stewart Udall

11

PLANNING FOR PARKS

The most effective way you can influence the future of national parks and their management is through the park planning process.

This has not always been the case. Prior to the 1970s, planning was rarely open to public involvement. The change occurred when the National Park Service crafted a master plan for Yosemite National Park that included a convention center and a tram to the top of Half Dome. Public outrage at the degree of commercial development planned for one of the country's most treasured landscapes forced NPS to scrap the plan.

In writing a new plan, the National Park Service responded to public interest by mailing more than 60,000 review drafts to individuals throughout the country. This massive effort remains the largest public involvement campaign ever instituted by NPS. But more importantly, it marked the beginning of regular opportunity for public involvement in NPS planning.

In 1978, Congress passed the National Parks and Recreation Act, requiring the National Park Service to prepare and regularly revise general management plans for each national park. The general management plan (GMP) describes a park's purpose and its resources and specifically outlines the strategies to be employed for the next five to ten years to achieve the park's objectives.

The National Park Service has developed a number of policies and guidelines that outline the planning needed for a park. In their guidelines, they state that planning is a "dynamic, continuous process for making choices about how to accomplish the National Park Service's preservation and enjoyment mandates." Furthermore, they specify that "opportunities will be provided for the public at the national, regional and local levels to voice their concerns about planning and management of parks…at the earliest possible stages in the planning process and before planning decisions have been made." (The overall planning policies are defined in *Management Policies, Department of the Interior, National Park Service, 1988.*)

Although public involvement in park planning is now policy, it is not always readily sought or encouraged. It is up to you to seek out opportunities to participate in any National Park Service planning efforts for your park.

How To Influence the Park Planning Process

It is important to make the Park Service aware of your interest in being involved in the planning process early on. Historically the National Park Service has demonstrated a great deal of resistance to making substantive changes to its parks' general management plans *after a draft has been completed.* The earlier you get involved, the greater the influence you will have on the final product.

- **Contact your park superintendent and ask the status of all planning for the park.** Although the park may not be engaged in a general management plan revision, it is probably developing some subordinate plans such as development concept plans or visitor management plans. Ask to be placed on the park's mailing list for planning notices.
- **Write and ask for the annual printout of all completed plans for your park.** This list is available from the Technical Information Center of the Denver Service Center, 12795 West Alameda Parkway, P.O. Box 25287, Denver, CO 80225-0287. This will serve as a confirmation of the information provided by the park.
- **Request that public scoping meetings be scheduled** and then participate when you learn that a

planning effort is being initiated.
- **Notify other groups or individuals** who are concerned with the park's preservation when you become aware of a planning effort.

The Planning Process

The planning process has five major stages: development of the statement for management, outline of planning requirements, identification of task directives, development of a general management plan, and development of implementation plans. The National Park Service has defined specific requirements for each phase of planning. It is useful to be familiar with the requirements when reviewing plans to identify where they might be deficient.

•Statement for Management

The Statement for Management (SFM) briefly describes the purpose of a park and provides an inventory of resource conditions and problems. It does not define strategies for problem resolution. The park's superintendent and staff are responsible for developing the SFM, but they may be assisted by other of-

At Maine's Acadia National Park, park advocates play an integral role in planning. Friends of Acadia's Duane Pierson is profiled on page 150.

fices. SFMs must be revised every two years.

The Park Service's first task in developing an SFM is to review the park's information base so as to define its *location, purpose* and *significance*, and the *influences* on it.

The park's location is described by a vicinity map and the official boundary map from the authorizing legislation. Its *purpose* is derived from the goals of resource preservation and public use stated in its enabling legislation. The *significance* of a park is determined by its resources. *Influences* on a park are to include factors both within and beyond its boundaries. These include:

- **Legislative and administrative requirements**—all authorizations, obligations, restrictions and commitments contained in legislative reports, hearing records and administrative documents pertaining to the park.

- **Resources**—all natural and cultural resources and the factors affecting their condition. (The quality of this information can vary with each park and should be carefully scrutinized to make sure it adequately accounts for *all* resources.)

- **Land-use trends**—an analysis of all land uses in and near the park and a listing of who owns these lands.

- **Visitor-use analysis**—an analysis of the recreational and nonrecreational visitation trends over the past 10 years, including information on how many people visited, and how they used, the park.

- **Facilities and equipment analysis**—the park's infrastructure, including roads and trails, buildings, utility and sewer systems, and major equipment such as automobiles and trucks.

- **Status of planning**—all plans and studies both completed or in progress.

- **Existing management zoning**—a map of current management zoning (natural, historic, park development, special use) that includes the park boundaries, significant natural and cultural resources, park developments, jurisdictions and other relevant features.

(It is important to check that all significant resources are included in appropriate zones.)

The most important product of the review of influences is the identification of the *major issues* facing the park. These issues define the management strategies developed throughout the planning process. The Statement for Management also should contain a list of management objectives that describe the "desired conditions" for the park, based on its purpose.

The draft Statement for Management is then reviewed and revised by the park's National Park Service regional office and other affected NPS offices before being made available for public comment. NPS policies on public review of the statement are determined on a case-by-case basis. A superintendent may determine that public notice in the local media and availability of review copies at the park may be sufficient.

Review of the Statement for Management is probably the part of the process that the public most ignores. Yet, you can have the greatest influence during this part because of the opportunity to provide input on how problems are defined. You should request in writing that the park staff notify you when an SFM is being developed (in the case of a new park) or revised (in the case of an existing unit) and that a copy of the draft be sent to you.

Following the public comment period, the Statement for Management is revised and approved by the regional director. National Park Service planning policy does not require public notification of changes unless they are significant or there is substantial public interest.

•Outline of Planning Requirements

Following the drafting of the Statement for Management, an Outline of Planning Requirements is prepared that identifies in sequence the planning, design and study needs for a park.

Requests for funding the various planning and study tasks are described and justified in development/study proposals known as form 10-238. These proposals annually undergo NPS regional review and approval.

•Task Directive

Once a task, such as the development of a GMP, has been approved, a written Task Directive is prepared that describes how the task is to be accomplished, which office is responsible, and the issues or problems to be addressed. This document should clearly indicate when and how the public will be involved in the planning process, and if an environmental impact statement or environmental assessment will be prepared.

The National Park Service may, but is not required to, "scope" out the issues of concern to the public prior to the development of a review draft of a plan. Scoping is often accomplished through the release of an "alternatives document" for public review. The decision as to whether to solicit public comment on alternatives is often determined by the Park Service's perception of public interest and potential controversy surrounding a proposed plan.

•General Management Plan/Environmental Document

This plan defines the park's management philosophy and prescribes management strategies to address issues for a five- to ten-year period. The two overriding purposes of the National Park Service—to preserve resources and to provide for the visitor's enjoyment—must be represented in the strategies. The park's effect on the region and the region's effect on the park also must be considered throughout the development of the plan. Most parks have either GMPs or the predecessor planning document that was known as a "master plan."

In 1978, Congress mandated that each park must have a GMP that "shall be prepared and revised in a timely manner." It further required that "GMPs shall include, but not be limited to":

- measures for the preservation of the area's resources;
- indications of types and general intensities of development (including visitor circulation and transportation patterns, systems and modes) associated with public enjoyment and use of the area, including general locations, timing of implementation and anticipated costs;
- identification of and implementation commitments for visitor carrying capacities for all areas of the unit (see Chapter 8 for more on carrying capacities);

• and indications of potential modifications to the external boundaries of the park (see Chapter 6 for more on park boundary adjustments).

Creating a GMP usually constitutes a major federal action. Therefore, an environmental impact statement or at least an environmental assessment is prepared according to the requirements of the National Environmental Policy Act. (See Chapter 13 for information on NEPA.)

There are five phases in the development of a general management plan. Phases 3 though 5 allow for your input:

- **Phase 1—Issue Analysis**
- **Phase 2—Development of Alternatives**
- **Phase 3—Alternative Document for Public Involvement**

This is an optional stage during which the National Park Service may "scope" public concerns. It is important that you encourage NPS to conduct scoping and that you participate in the process. Because the decision to involve the public must have the approval of the NPS regional director, you should send a copy of any written requests for scoping to the regional director for your park. Emphasize any or all of these in your request:

- The issues and the alternatives are controversial.
- The public and other interested officials are expected to be in disagreement with NPS alternatives.
- The alternatives will significantly affect the social and economic life of nearby communities.
- User groups may be curtailed in their use of the park, or new uses may be permitted that are controversial.
- Boundary adjustments may be proposed that would affect adjacent land uses.
- The cost of the plan is expected to be high.
- The resource protection and use issues are significant.

The alternatives document should contain a summary of the information in the Statement for Management and a concise description of alternatives. Frequently the Park Service uses mail questionnaires as its scoping instrument, but public hearings are also employed. When you submit your comments, ask that you receive the draft general management plan when it is available.

Profile: Duane Pierson

Duane Pierson will be the first to admit that he doesn't mind having a few Rockefeller family members and over a dozen more Fortune 500 types on his board of trustees. But as president of Friends of Acadia—a private support organization for Maine's Acadia National Park—the 56-year-old Pierson hasn't lost sight of his group's basic mission: to become an "equal partner" with the National Park Service in its management of 40,000 acres of parklands off Maine's Mount Desert Island.

Five years ago, Pierson says, the park's 250 miles of sculptured trails and carriage roads were badly deteriorating and public criticism of park management was mounting. A small group of longtime park advocates sought an outsider who could turn things around, and it was Pierson who showed up at their doorstep in 1989.

A former environmental science professor at the State University of New York in Fredonia (and the director, subsequently, of two wildlife conservation organizations), Pierson joined the group in its seat-of-the-pants beginnings. Friends of Acadia, founded with 150 members in 1986, has grown to over 3,000 members, and what Pierson originally envisioned as an ideal part-time job in a beautiful park that would support another career as a writer—Pierson has written two novels—has blossomed into full-time stewardship of one of the most powerful private park advocacy groups in the country.

Friends of Acadia supports a 21-member Board of Directors, an equal number of trustees, several committees dedicated to park policy-making and plenty of field troops. A broad coalition ranging from high school students and fishermen to a core of older summer residents, many of whom grew up around the park, Friends of Acadia contributes over 25,000 hours of volunteer labor each year. The group's popular summer youth program employs high-school students who help clear trails and maintain carriage roads.

From clearing brush to cultivating friends and dollars in their congressional delegation, Friends of Acadia, Pierson says, "does everything for the park it can't do for itself."

Friends of Acadia under Pierson's direction has become a model for the potential role citizens can play in modern park management. After decades of passive, institutional control by the federal government, friends groups like Acadia's are stepping in to play direct roles—and serving a watchdog function as well—in issues such as visitor management, overdevelopment, park planning and environmental protection—all problems the National Park Service, Pierson believes, can no longer manage on its own.

Unlike the National Park Service, he says, the friends group "shuns consensus management approaches to problems as being unproductive and tremendously time consuming. We are a leadership management organization—very action- and result-oriented."

"Being a government bureaucracy," Pierson explains, "the Park Service moves very slowly on things such as visitor control and quality-of-life issues we think are important. We push them to move faster—and what they don't do, we try to go out and accomplish ourselves." Although Acadia's operations will always be the domain of Park Service employees, Friends of Acadia has made itself an unavoidable—but cooperative—presence in the shadow of federal authority. The group's standing committees meet face-to-face with park managers on everything from drafting general management plans to electing new park superintendents.

Away from their dealings with park managers, Pierson's organization has lobbied and won Congressional support for a $10 million restoration of the park's carriage road system and raised $4 million on its own for a permanent park maintenance fund.

Not all national parks have Acadia's advantages—chief among them the relative wealth and involvement of its neighbors. As Pierson points out, "We're lucky to be surrounded by a strong local community with a long tradition of volunteerism, and we have access to funding that other parks can't get because they're so isolated." Remote areas like Glacier National Park, Pierson points out, "have no local constituencies except those that are semi-hostile, like logging interests or ranchers."

After five years of success in battling against institutional resistance, Pierson has advice for fledgling groups now sprouting up in parks around the country. "You can't be intimidated by park management," Pierson warns. "You have to be a little more assertive and stronger—not in a nasty-minded, adversarial sense—but the managers need to understand that you are bringing something to them, and you want to be treated as equal partners, working together with mutual interests."

Pierson and friends often find the path to park management as rocky as the crushed-stone carriage roads Acadia is known for. "We keep a good relationship [with the Park Service], but I know we're a very credible force—they have to reckon with it."

•Phase 4—Preparation of Draft GMP

Once the draft plan is prepared, it is reviewed within the National Park Service by the park and regional staffs, the Washington NPS office and (when combined with an environmental document) the solicitor's office. Plans that are considered controversial are also reviewed by the office of the Assistant Secretary for Fish, Wildlife and Parks.

Upon completion of any revisions, the plan is released to the public for review by the NPS regional office for a minimum of 30 days. Plans that are accompanied by an EIS must allow 60 days for public review. The availability of the plan is usually announced in local newspapers and in the *Federal Register* if accompanied by an environmental document. Public workshops and meetings may be conducted to discuss the draft GMP, particularly if it is controversial. If you have notified the park staff in writing of your interest in the plan, you should receive either the plan itself or a notice of its availability in the mail.

•Phase 5—Preparation and Approval of the Plan

During this phase, the planning team makes adjustments to the plan based upon the comments they've received. If the changes are within the scope of the proposal, the plan is released to the public for a 30-day review prior to final approval by the regional director. The National Park Service is very reluctant to make changes to a final plan and will do so only if it determines that new information has been brought forward that sufficiently challenges the plan's proposed actions.

If the changes made to the draft GMP are beyond the scope of the actions originally proposed, a supplemental draft GMP may be prepared and released for public review.

•Implementation Plans

The general management plan can be supplemented by a number of more focused implementing plans. These may include a resources management plan, an interpretive prospectus or a land protection plan. Depending upon the resources of a park, other, more specialized plans may be developed, including fire management plans, visitor management plans and exotic species control plans.

Chapter 12

Park Laws, Regulations and Policies

The heart of our movement [the park movement] is a thing of the spirit, although the material we deal with is land. It is a high calling that has as its purpose to assure the people of the future that they will have have the great experiences in the out-of-doors that we have had.

Newton B. Drury

12

PARK LAWS, REGULATIONS AND POLICIES

Many statutes, regulations, executive orders and policies govern the administration, protection and use of the National Park System. As a park advocate, you should understand the legal framework upon which the management and use of your park are based. Participation in legal processes, such as formulation of regulations, can be key in park protection and management.

At times, because of an action the National Park Service takes or fails to take, NPS may be in violation of its legal responsibilities. An adjacent landowner or another federal agency may take actions that pose a threat to park resources. After you have exhausted administrative opportunities for correcting the situation, you may need to explore legal action to force NPS to take what you believe is the appropriate action. Oftentimes, lawyers may donate legal assistance for cases involving park protection on a *pro bono* basis.

While this chapter does not attempt to outline each step necessary in filing a lawsuit, it does discuss the legal framework that parks operate within and how to find representation should you wish to pursue a legal action.

What You Need To Know

It is important to be familiar with the body of laws, regulations and policies that specifically affect your park. It is also important to be aware and active when there are changes proposed to those laws, regulations and policies.

- Request a copy of the park's enabling act and associated regulations from the park's superintendent. It would also be useful to get a copy of the legislative history for the enabling act because it gives further insight into the intent of Congress when it established the park.
- Ask the park staff whether any changes are anticipated for those laws and regulations.
- Request that you be notified whenever a change is proposed in park regulations or policy.
- Obtain a copy of the National Park Service's Management Policies by writing to the Office of Policy, National Park Service, U.S. Department of Interior, Washington, D.C. 20240.
- Obtain a copy of any NPS guidelines pertinent to issues you are following in your park.

Laws

Laws created by legislatures to declare, command or prohibit something are statutes. Most of the laws guiding the management and use of the parks are statutes. Laws that have been derived from court decisions and are based upon usage or custom are common laws. General principles of nuisance law are derived from common law.

Some statutes address the park system in general. The overarching law governing activities of the National Park Service is the National Park Service Organic Act (see page 157 for more on the Organic Act).

Other statutes are specific to individual parks. The majority of parks were established by individual acts of Congress.

The management and use of national parks are also influenced by general federal environmental statutes, such as the Clean Air Act and the National Environmental Policy Act, which have sweeping provisions that affect a wide variety of federal programs and activities.

Additionally, there are laws that establish other resource systems—wilderness, scenic and historic trails, and wild and scenic rivers—that give the Park Service additional authorities and responsibilities beyond those established in the general and specific park laws and the federal environmental laws.

If you are interested in looking up a law and its amendments, check your local library. Many libraries have a copy of the United States Code, which contains the federal laws concerning parks and the environment. (An alphabetical list of key laws and executive orders affecting parks appears in the appendices.)

Generic Park Laws

• **The Organic Act** *(16 USC § 1):*

Congress began creating national parks in 1872 with the establishment of Yellowstone National Park. It was not until the passage of the National Park Service Organic Act in 1916, however, that Congress created the National Park Service to manage these parks as a system. The Act declared that NPS had a dual mission, both to *conserve parks' resources* and to *provide for their use and enjoyment* "in such a manner and by such means as will leave them unimpaired for future generations."

The Act, which has been amended over the years, is the primary legal source of NPS's protection of its parks. Although the law is decades old, the meaning of some of its provisions is still being debated. In particular, there has been tension between providing for the use and enjoyment of national parks and the responsibility of the Park Service to protect the parks and leave them "unimpaired" for future generations.

• **The General Authorities Act of 1970** *(16 USC § 1a-1):*

Two of the most significant amendments to the Organic Act are in the 1970 General Authorities Act and the 1978 Redwoods National Park Expansion Act. The General Authorities Act amendment declared that "...though distinct in character, [national parks] are united through their interrelated purposes and resources into one National Park System as cumulative expressions of a single national heritage."

In the decades between the passage of the Organic Act and this amendment, the National Park System had come to include many diverse types of parks, such as national seashores and battlefield memorials, each with its own set of purposes and authorities. The significance of this amendment was to clarify that all parks are united under the mission, purposes and protection of the Organic Act unless Congress specifically states otherwise.

• **Redwoods Act Amendment** *(16 USC § 1a-1):*

In 1978, when Congress expanded Redwood National Park to protect its resources from the effects of logging outside the park, it chose to include an amendment to the Organic Act which stated that all park management activities shall be:

...conducted in light of the high public value and integrity of the National Park System and shall not be exercised in derogation of the values and purposes for which these various areas have been established, except as may have been or shall be directly and specifically provided for by Congress.

Although the protection authorized by this provision has not been tested in court, it is generally agreed that the intent of Congress in adding this amendment to the Organic Act was to ensure that the values for which a park was established are protected—unless Congress determines otherwise.

Park-Specific Laws

Most parks were established by Congress. The statute that establishes a park is known as its enabling act. A park can also be established by a presidential proclamation or executive order under the authority of the Antiquities Act of 1906. Zion National Park is one example of a park originally created by presidential proclamation.

The primary purpose for the establishment of a park is contained in its enabling act or proclamation. This purpose might be the protection of unique geological or scenic features or the preservation of a site which has historical or cultural value. For example, Sitka National Historical Park in Alaska preserves the site of the 1804 fort and battle that marked the last major Tlingit Indian resistance to Russian colonization.

An enabling act also defines a park's boundaries. Most enabling acts also include an authorization for appropriations. This is supposed to represent the total amount Congress is willing to spend on completing a park. Congress must still appropriate the money on a yearly basis.

Continuation of pre-existing activities such as grazing or

Zion National Park, one of the few parks established by presidential procla-mation under the authority of the Antiquities Act of 1906.

mining may also be permitted by the enabling act. For example, 16 USC § 406d-2 authorizes grazing in Grand Teton National Park. Hunting, fishing, and subsistence-use issues are often addressed in enabling legislation. An example of this type of provision is found in 16 USC § 410h-2, which allows hunting in national preserves in Alaska.

Copies of the enabling act for a park should be available from the park superintendent. Most of the enabling acts are codified in Title 16 of the United States Code.

General Laws That Affect National Parks

The management of the National Park System is also governed by a variety of general environmental laws. Below are the most significant.

•**Clean Air Act** *(PL 88-206 as amended, 42 USC § 7401 et seq.)*

This law establishes programs to improve and maintain safe and acceptable ambient air quality. It sets specific goals for cleaning up areas of the country with dirty air and protecting areas with pristine air quality such as national parks. (For further discussion, see Chapter 10, "Protecting Park Air Quality.")

•**Freedom of Information Act** *(PL 93-502, 5 USC § 552 et seq.)*

This is an important law for park advocates because it requires government agencies to make their information available to the public. Agencies may deny requests for information when it concerns national security, internal agency rules and memoranda, trade secrets, personal privacy, investigatory records, or is exempted by another federal statute.

Agencies are required to respond to Freedom of Information Act requests within 10 working days of the initial request but frequently extend the deadline. If a response is not received by the deadline, an appeal may be filed. Agencies may charge fees for the search and duplication of materials, so be exact in your requests. For further information on the Freedom of Information Act, write to the Freedom of Information Clearinghouse, P.O. Box 19367, Washington, D.C. 20036.

•**Land and Water Conservation Fund Act, 1964** *(PL 88-578, 16 USC § 460l et seq.)*

This Act establishes a fund for the planning and purchase of outdoor recreation areas and facilities. Appropriations from the Fund may be made by Congress for allocation to: 1) states, on a matching basis, for planning, acquisition of land and water areas, and for construction of outdoor recreation facilities; 2) federal agencies, including the National Park Service, for use in acquiring land needed for outdoor recreation. Revenue for the Fund now comes principally from off-shore oil leases, with additional revenue from a few minor sources. Today, about $900 million a year is going into the Fund, but actual appropriations are nowhere near this amount. Legislation in 1987 extended the Fund through 2015. (For further information, see Chapter 14, "Congress and The Park System.")

• **National Environmental Policy Act** *(PL 91-190, 42 USC § 4321 et seq.)*

The leading federal environmental statute, the National Environmental Policy Act (NEPA), requires federal agencies to use a systematic, interdisciplinary approach to planning to determine if proposed federal actions will have a significant effect on the environment. It requires public involvement in the planning process and the development of alternatives prior to any final action. (For further information, see Chapter 13, "The National Environmental Policy Act.")

• **The Wilderness Act of 1964** *(PL 88-577 16 USC § 1311 et seq.)*

This Act gives Congress the authority to designate certain federal lands as "wilderness." The areas must be primitive and "untrammeled" or undeveloped by humans. One of the purposes of wilderness is to provide areas of sufficient size to permit unconfined recreational activities such as hiking and horseback riding. The National Park Service is one of the four land-managing agencies charged to manage these areas under the Act. Except in situations where prior rights exist, a number of activities are prohibited in wilderness areas, including construction and road development, oil and gas drilling, mining and logging.

Regulations

Following the passage of a law pertaining to parks, the National Park Service drafts a series of regulations to implement the provisions of the law. In general, these regulations are only as specific as the laws on which they are based.

The federal Administrative Procedures Act (5 USC § 551, *et seq.*) controls the National Park Service's rule-making proceedings. It also governs when a rule may be appealed in federal court. Unless NPS finds that the situation merits emergency regulations, the Act requires that the public must be notified of their intention to propose regulations and be given an opportunity to comment on the regulations before they are finalized.

Usually, the public is asked to file written comments on proposed regulations. NPS may also decide to hold a public hearing. The length of time that NPS will accept comments can vary depending on the complexity of the regulations, but generally it ranges from 30 to 60 days. If your comments are not ready in this time period, you can ask the Park Service for an extension.

In the event that a situation needs immediate attention, the National Park Service can issue "emergency regulations" that take effect immediately, even though they remain open to public comment.

Draft, final and emergency regulations, as well as changes in regulations, are announced in the *Federal Register*. The Park Service also sends out announcements to individuals and groups they know to be interested. Be sure to write to your park officials and tell them of your intention to comment on any proposed regulations that may affect your park.

It is important to comment on as many proposed regulations that will affect your park as you can. You can suggest ways to improve the proposed regulations or you can state your opposition to them. State your case as clearly as possible. An argument for or against a particular position may seem obvious to you, but include it in your comments anyway.

If you are aware of inconsistency between the position the National Park Service has taken in the past and the position it is taking in the proposed regulations, be sure to point it out. For example, NPS recently proposed exempting Rock Creek Park's tennis stadium from NPS regulations prohibiting commercial advertising in NPS units. The National Parks and Conservation Association argued that there should be no exemptions from the well-reasoned policies originally articulated in support of the commercial ban. Unfortunately, NPS granted the exemption.

In cases where you find the regulations are satisfactory, it is important to declare your support for them. Although the National Park Service doesn't base its regulations on a popularity poll, comments received on proposals often do affect the outcome of the process. If the regulation is opposed by other parties, NPS needs to be able to point to some support for the proposal.

The National Park Service's general body of regulations cover a wide range of activities such as hunting, picnicking and concessions operations. They are contained in Volume 36 of the *Code of Federal Regulations* (CFR). Periodically, the National Park Service comprehensively updates these general regulations. The *Code of Federal Regulations* can be found in law libraries and public reserve libraries.

Each park can also issue regulations specific to activities occurring within its boundaries, such as snowmobile use or fishing. These also, for the most part, can be found in Volume 36 of CFR. Each park should have a complete body of the regulations pertaining to its operation available for public review.

Policies and Guidelines

Policies set the framework and provide direction for management decisions. The National Park Service has developed extensive policies that govern everything from planning to concessions management. As with regulations, they are periodically updated. NPS publishes its management policies in a single book, which may be obtained by writing to the NPS Office of Policy, U.S. Department of Interior, Washington, D.C. 20240.

While policies are based on law, they can be subject to shifts in the political winds. In the early 1980s, during the Reagan Administration, the National Park Service's policies toward land acquisition were changed from advocating full-fee purchase of unacquired land within authorized park boundaries to advocating other protection measures such as zoning and easements.

Guidelines specifically outline how NPS should address various aspects of managing the parks. They are extensions and elaborations of the provisions set down in the laws and policies.

Executive Orders

An executive order is a directive from the President to a federal agency, such as the Department of the Interior. One of the most significant executive orders affecting the parks is E.O. 11644 (42 FR 26959), which requires that specific zones be established for off-road-vehicle use on federal lands. This order has resulted in restrictions of off-road-vehicle use on parklands.

Taking Legal Action

If you believe that you or your group has a cause for action against the National Park Service or some other agency or individual, you should seek legal representation so that you can bring a case to court. Most individual park advocates or small groups do not have the resources to retain an attorney. There are opportunities, however, to obtain *pro bono* or reduced-fee legal counsel.

To obtain *pro bono* assistance, you must be able to state your case clearly. You may not necessarily be able to describe the legal authorities you could rely on in court but, generally, the more clearly you describe the problem, the easier it is to interest someone in helping you. You should have all the relevant documents together so that you can send them quickly if someone appears interested in helping you. There are usually deadlines for filing an action, and you do not want to waste any time.

Some national environmental groups provide legal services to groups or individuals if the case involves an environmental issue. An example of such a group is the Sierra Club Legal Defense Fund, headquartered in San Francisco. Other legal environmental groups focus on more regional issues. An example is the Southern Environmental Law Center, with offices in Virginia and North Carolina.

Often a law school will have professors interested in environmental law who handle important cases for groups or individuals. Some law schools have clinics focusing on litigation or the environment where law students assist professors in handling cases. For example, the Georgetown University Law Center has a legal clinic, the Institute for Public Interest Representation, that focuses on urban environmental problems among other issues.

Law school professors are an important resource for you to consider in searching for an attorney. Even if there is no professor willing to take your case, professors can often recommend lawyers in your state who may be familiar with the issues involved in your case.

Private attorneys are another possibility. Many law firms provide *pro bono* assistance to a variety of groups. Most bar associations encourage their members to provide public service. Most firms fulfill their public service obligations by providing free legal assistance to worthy causes and individuals.

The local bar association may be able to help you locate private attorneys willing to assist you with your case. Often the bar association has lists of attorneys willing to take *pro bono* cases and their areas of expertise and interest.

To obtain *pro bono* assistance, call the firm and ask for the person in charge of *pro bono* assistance. Describe the situation in as much detail as you can and the firm will decide whether it will take the case. Factors a firm will consider in reaching their decision include any potential conflicts with paying clients, the firm's overall work load and whether an individual in the firm is interested in handling the case.

Many public interest law firms represent nonprofit groups at reduced rates. Your local bar association may have a listing of these.

It is important to have a clear understanding of the agreement with the attorney representing you. You may be required to sign a retainer agreement that outlines your responsibilities. Even if an organization or individual attorney will not charge you for legal fees, you may be required to pay expenses associated with the case. Depending on the case, these costs can be substantial. For example, your case may require the testimony of an expert witness such as a wildlife biologist. Expert witnesses often charge fees, but it is also possible to find an expert willing to testify *pro bono* or at a reduced rate.

Chapter 13

The National Environmental Policy Act

The state of civilization of a people may be measured by its care and forethought for the welfare of generations to come.

Dr. John C. Merriam

13

THE NATIONAL ENVIRONMENTAL POLICY ACT

Of all the laws enacted to protect this nation's environmental resources, including its national parks, perhaps none is more important than the National Environmental Policy Act (NEPA). It is a law that has revolutionized resource protection and planning not only in this country, but throughout the world.

Signed into law on January 1, 1970, NEPA requires federal agencies to "utilize a systematic, interdisciplinary approach which will insure the integrated use of the natural and social sciences and environmental design arts in planning and decision-making which may have an impact on man's environment." It mandates that agencies recognize the environmental impacts of their projects and provide alternatives and mitigation options prior to making a decision.

More importantly, it has institutionalized public participation and agency consideration of alternatives. Because NEPA requires the release of basic resource information to the public, it brings new and unexamined perspectives to an issue. When it comes to the National Park System, NEPA fosters opportunities for NPS professionals and citizens to become partners in the work of protecting the parks by allowing for early involvement in the planning process.

This is not to say that the National Park Service always welcomes public involvement with open arms. At times, NEPA compliance has been viewed by NPS managers as an obstacle, a bureaucratic exercise or a challenge to implementing a predetermined decision. Regardless of whatever resistance you or your group may be met with, bear in mind that NEPA insures that it is your legal right, not privilege, to be involved in the decision-making process affecting your park. Understanding NEPA can provide you with a powerful tool as an advocate for your park.

The NEPA Process

In 1978, the Council on Environmental Quality (CEQ) issued final regulations for the implementation of NEPA. A copy of these regulations (40 CFR 1500-1508) and a list of the "40 Most Asked Questions About NEPA" may be obtained by writing to CEQ, 722 Jackson Place N.W., Washington, D.C. 20503.

The National Park Service's informal NEPA Compliance Guidelines provide additional interpretation of the NEPA regulations as they pertain to NPS, but they do not have the force of law. To obtain a copy, contact the Environmental Compliance Division of any NPS regional headquarters.

Any National Park Service action is subject to NEPA. The Park Service's Environmental Review program and NPS compliance with NEPA is handled by the Environmental Quality Division. Based in Washington, the Environmental Quality Division is responsible for distributing documents to the appropriate NPS office for review. It also coordinates the NPS response to a NEPA document, which may involve coordinating comments from several regions and NPS divisions.

The degree to which the National Park System initially documents and analyzes potential environmental impacts may vary with its perception of the significance of the action. There are essentially three levels of documentation: categorical exclusions, environmental assessments and environmental impact statements.

•Categorical Exclusions

Many of the routine activities of federal agencies do not pose an individual or cumulative threat to the environment. They are classified as categorical exclusions and do not require further analysis or documentation. National Park Service guidelines define which actions will normally be given categorical exclusions

including activities related to:
- general administration—such as renewal of permits, routine maintenance and repair;
- plans, studies and reports—such as land-acquisition and boundary surveys and interpretive plans;
- and development that does not affect the environment—such as paving a turnout area on a paved road and putting a picnic table near it.

The National Park Service does have exceptions to activities that are normally classed as categorical exclusions if they have uncertain or significant impact on the environment, public health and safety, endangered species or areas of natural, historic or cultural value. Exception may also be taken if the action sets a potentially threatening precedent, could be harmful in tandem with other actions, or violates a federal, state, local or tribal law.

A manager's decision to class an action as a categorical exclusion is often not reviewed by higher authorities and the potential for abuse is great. Local park advocates must maintain a constant vigil to ensure that actions that deserve an environmental impact statement or at least an environmental assessment do not slip through the cracks. For example, the National Park Service recently transferred NPS lands to the government of the District of Columbia to facilitate development of a theme park without any review under NEPA.

•Environmental Assessments

If there is any evidence that the proposed action could result in a significant environmental impact, an environmental assessment (EA) may be prepared. An EA briefly explains the need for the proposal, alternatives to the proposal, as well as the environmental, cultural and socio-economic impacts of the proposal. It also gives a list of the agencies and individuals consulted in its formulation.

Prior to issuance of a final environmental assessment, the agency must give the public an opportunity to comment on the document. There is usually a 30-day review period, although this may vary according to public interest or special circumstances surrounding the proposal.

An environmental assessment results in either a "finding of no significant impact" or a determination to prepare an environmental impact statement. With national park actions, it is left to the superintendent's discretion whether to announce the decision in the *Federal Register.* Usually superintendents do not have the decision printed, which means it is doubly important for you to have regular communication with your superintendent on the status of such decisions.

•Environmental Impact Statements

The most in-depth analysis of the environmental consequences of a proposed action is developed in an environmental impact statement (EIS). Federal agencies regularly seek to avoid preparing EISs because of the time and expense. As John Donohue wrote in the National Park Service *Courier* in June of 1990, "Although NEPA may be a four-letter word in many circles, it is really those three little letters 'EIS' that strike fear into the hearts of managers and planners."

The vast majority of lawsuits involving NEPA pertain to agency failure to adhere to Section 102's requirement that the lead agency file an environmental impact statement "for each federal action significantly affecting the human environment."

According to its own guidelines, NPS will at a minimum prepare an environmental assessment, but usually will prepare an EIS for the following:

- Wild and Scenic River proposals
- National Trail proposals
- Wilderness proposals
- General management plans for major national parks (probably the most frequent reason the Park Service prepares an EIS)
- Grants, including multi-year grants, whose size and/ or scope will result in major natural or physical changes, including interrelated social and economic changes and residential and land-use changes within the project area or its immediate environs
- Grants which foreclose other beneficial uses of mineral, agricultural, timber, water, energy or transportation resources important to national or state welfare

•How an EIS Is Prepared

The lead agency in the proposed action files a notice in the *Federal Register* when it is planning to prepare an EIS. The next phase—"scoping" or identification of the key issues related to the proposed action—is where you can have the greatest impact on the process. Public meetings in the vicinity of the affected national park, and, in the case of nationally controversial actions, throughout the country, are the typical means by which NPS conducts scoping. The Park Service guidelines explain that:

Scoping is a process and not simply a single event or meeting, although scoping meetings are sometimes held. Public participation may provide input to the scoping process, but is not the only element of it. The scoping process sifts all input for critical environmental significance, decides upon the issues and alternatives to be documented in the EIS and provides the reasons for dropping lesser environmental issues and alternatives from further consideration.

Scoping is when issues are raised and problems identified. If you wait until the EIS process is completed before voicing concern, the Park Service is likely to turn a deaf ear, and your chances for establishing "standing" in a legal challenge will be substantially lessened.

During scoping you can request that certain alternatives are considered and that specific data are collected or studies completed. The fulfillment of the data gathering requirements of NEPA should enhance a park's baseline data collection and monitoring. If you oppose the proposed action, it is important that you be well-armed with data or at least be prepared to request that the type of data that could support your position be gathered.

An important request to make during scoping is that all impacts be assessed against the "nonimpairment" mandate of the National Park Service's Organic Act. The Act and its amendments require that park resources be "preserved *unimpaired* for future generations" and that management of park system areas "shall not be exercised in derogation of the values and purposes for which these areas have been established." (See page 157 for more discussion of the Organic Act.)

Furthermore, it is important to request that an adequate analysis be prepared of the potential *cumulative* impacts upon the park. A series of apparently minor impacts often combines to cause or contribute to major problems in parks. Each impact is not an isolated event but one drip into an ever-deepening pool. For example, three separate EISs were necessary to address the cumulative impacts on mining near Alaska parks. The National Park Service looked at the whole region in terms of water quality, caribou habitat and air quality.

After analyzing the results of the scoping process, the agency issues a draft EIS. It is supposed to feature a scientifically accurate description of the affected environment, a detailed explanation of the action the agency wants to take, an assessment of how the environment will be affected, and a description of mitigating measures.

It is especially important to take a close look at draft EISs as, frequently, agencies have attempted to subvert the scoping process to reflect their own position. William Penn Mott, the former Director of the National Park Service, noted, "Too often, we (at NPS) have all seen...situations where a course of action is decided and an attempt is made to tailor the environmental analysis to the decision. This invites environmentally unsound actions, delays needed to take corrective action, and public distrust of agency goals and motives."

Public comment on a draft, submitted in writing, is usually accepted for 60 days, although an extension is often granted for a large, complex draft EIS. Agencies are supposed to carefully consider public comment when making their final decision on the proposed action. Substantive written comments are appended to the final EIS along with the Park Service's response. This gives the agency an opportunity to provide further explanation of the rationale behind its decision, and it gives you an opportunity to identify other issues should you ultimately take legal action.

When reviewing a draft EIS, you should analyze the adequacy of the information and determine if the alternative most protective of your park has been addressed. Evaluate the draft's consistency with other plans and policies, such as general management plans, statements for management and management policies. Collaborating with other park activists and environmental groups can help to strengthen your position on the proposed action with the Park Service.

•Record of Decision

Following the issuance of a final decision on the proposed action, the agency is required to file a record of decision that explains how the environmental considerations were factored into the decision. It describes the alternatives considered, the environmentally preferred alternative, and, if it is different, the agency's preferred alternative. It is a useful document for courts to use in determining if the agency decision was "arbitrary and capricious."

•Proposed Actions By Other Agencies

Often it is the action of other federal agencies that pose a threat to your park. For example, the U.S. Forest Service may be planning a timber cut on land adjacent to the park that would affect park waterways or the Federal Highway Administration may be providing funds for a new roadway that will bisect an ecosystem important to the park. (See Chapter 5, "Protecting Parks from External Threats.")

The National Park Service does a better job than most federal agencies in the preparation of EISs and EAs, but has not been as successful when it comes to effectively using the NEPA process to deal with external threats arising from projects initiated by other agencies.

Not only is it important for you to participate in scoping and to prepare written comments, but you should also monitor and encourage strong National Park Service involvement as well. The best opportunity the National Park Service has to influence another agency's NEPA process is to become a cooperating agency. As a cooperating agency, NPS has responsibility to participate in scoping and to provide environmental analysis. When NPS is designated a cooperating agency, you should demand that it prepare the assessment of potential impacts to park resources and values for the lead agency.

Regardless of National Park Service participation in another agency's NEPA process, it is important for you to participate. It will establish your standing or right to file a motion if a legal challenge to the agency's decision is necessary. Although NPS does have the option to refer a decision to the Council on Environmental Quality, as described below, NPS is not in a position to file a suit to stop another federal agency's actions.

CEQ Mediation

When the alternatives being proposed by, or the final decision of, another agency conflicts with the National Park Service's ability to protect park resources, you should encourage the Park Service to seek a referral to the Council on Environmental Quality for mediation. The Council attempts to bring the concerned agencies to the bargaining table to reconcile their differences, but its final recommendation is not legally binding.

There are a number of criteria that agencies use when deciding to refer a decision:
- possible violation of national environmental standards or policies
- severity of impact
- geographic scope of impact
- duration of impact
- importance as a precedent
- availability of environmentally preferable alternatives

There are two legal routes by which referrals may be made. A federal agency may refer a proposed major action to the CEQ 25 days after the final document has been released to the public or it may refer an action under Section 309 of the Clean Air Act, which allows the EPA administrator to refer any proposed federal action deemed to be environmentally unsatisfactory.

There is a 25-day period following CEQ's receipt of the referral during which the lead agency and the public are permitted to submit comments on the proposed action. This is another opportunity for you to voice your opinion on the proposed action.

According to J. William Futrell, writing in *Our Common Lands*, the effectiveness of the CEQ referral process in protecting park resources gets mixed reviews. It was instrumental in preventing the construction of a massive beach restoration by the U.S. Army Corps of Engineers at Fire Island National Seashore that would have devastated the unit's resources. However, a CEQ-mediated agreement to limit airport expansion at Grand Teton National Park in the late '70s was easily undercut by James Watt when he was Secretary of Interior in the early 1980s.

President Bill Clinton has proposed the abolition of CEQ as a cost-cutting measure. This action is not final at this time and is vigorously opposed by many park advocates. The Administration claims that another mechanism for fulfilling this CEQ function will be put in place.

Chapter 14

Congress and the Park System

Never doubt that a small group of thoughtful citizens can change the world; indeed, it is the only thing that ever has.

Margaret Mead

14

CONGRESS AND THE PARK SYSTEM

The National Park System and its managing agency, the National Park Service, are, for the most part, creations of Congress. By acts of Congress, new park areas are established, existing park boundaries are redrawn, and lands are added to preserve and enhance existing parks. Furthermore, nearly all funding for the National Park Service to acquire and manage national parklands is provided through the congressional appropriations process. In recent years, Congress typically has considered more than 100 pieces of park-related legislation in each two-year period. Because Congress plays such a large role in the establishment and maintenance of the National Park System, it is vital that park advocates be familiar with the legislative process.

How to Influence Legislation

The passage of even noncontroversial legislation requires a lot of time and dedication by its proponents. Ideally, parks and wilderness bills should have the support of the representative whose district is affected, both the U.S. senators from the affected state and, if appropriate, the support of local and state government. However, among the most important components of any legislative strategy is local community support. Often it is the work of the grassroots organizations and citizen activists that makes the difference in having a bill enacted.

Below we describe a generic 11-step strategy for influencing legislative process. (See Chapter 6 for specific information on pursuing boundary adjustments.) You should consult with an established conservation group when pursuing any legislative action. Thorough consultation and strategizing are always useful steps in launching a legislative campaign.

Step 1: Develop adequate information to justify your position on a legislative proposal. This is especially important for garnering congressional interest and support. Such information would include fact sheets, maps (if appropriate), and expert opinions. Develop arguments to counter any expected opposition.

Step 2: Solicit support for your proposal from as many diverse interests as possible. This demonstrates the broad-based appeal of the proposal. Encourage supporters to write to their representatives and senators. Begin to use the media in getting the word out on your proposal (see Chapter 4, "Telling Your Story to the News Media").

Step 3: Ask your representative and senators to introduce your proposal as legislation. Be willing to assist in drafting the actual legislation.

Step 4: Solicit congressional co-sponsors. It is especially important to garner co-sponsors from your state's congressional delegation and from the House Natural Resources and Senate Energy and Natural Resources committees. For a list of the members of these committees, refer to congressional directories usually available at your public library. (Prior to contacting congressional offices, read about the representatives and senators you have targeted in one of the several political almanacs available at the library.) Another good source of information on a legislator's environmental interests is the League of Conservation Voters, which rates legislators according to their environmental voting record. Try to get national groups to encourage their members to write to Congress in support of the legislation. Send thank-you letters to all legislators who become co-sponsors. Contact committee staff (ideally in person) to brief them on the proposal and identify any possible obstacles on the committee.

Step 5: Seek a public hearing. Ask your representative or senator to request a formal public hearing on the introduced bill.

Step 6: Request an opportunity to testify when a hearing is scheduled. Encourage other supporters to do the same. Provide a detailed written statement, but do not read it when testifying. Instead be prepared to make more concise oral remarks that focus on the overriding need for the legislation and that respond to any comments made by previous witnesses. Prior to the hearing, notify the local press of the date and time. Prepare a news release for the media.

Step 7: Encourage co-sponsors of the legislation to request a "markup." If there are major obstacles or concerns with the legislation, offer to work with committee staff to come up with satisfactory alternative language that achieves your goals. Develop and distribute information packets on the legislation to all members of the committee. Such packets should include information that addresses any opposition to the legislation. Make contact either by phone or in person with staff of committee members and request support for the legislation during "markup" (see page 186). Encourage other supporters whose members sit on the committee to again express their support for the legislation. The day before the markup, remind representatives/senators who are co-sponsors and any other obvious supporters who sit on the committee that the bill is coming up before the committee and that their vote is needed.

Step 8: Send thank-you letters to all members who voted in support of your position. Ask for their continued support on the floor. If the legislation was initially marked up in subcommittee (as is custom in the House), repeat step 7 for the full committee.

Step 9: Determine when the legislation is scheduled for floor action. The committee staff should know the legislative schedule.

Step 10: Develop and distribute an information packet to the full House or Senate. Encourage supporters to ask their representatives or senators to vote in favor of the bill. Notify supportive press of the bill's impending vote and encourage favorable editorials.

Step 11: Send thank-yous to the bill's sponsor, co-sponsors and any staff if it is passed. Such courtesy keeps the door open for other legislative opportunities.

The Legislative Process

Measures that affect the National Park System (such as a bill to designate a new park area or a bill to expand the boundaries of a park) are typically introduced in the House of Representatives by the representative whose congressional district is host to the park, or in the Senate by one or both of the senators from the state in which the park is located. A bill may be introduced simultaneously in both chambers to speed its passage. Although it is most often the case that a park bill is introduced by the park's U.S. representative, there are no restrictions on this and any member of Congress may choose to introduce legislation affecting any park.

When a bill is introduced, a representative may ask colleagues to "co-sponsor" the legislation. This means that other members of Congress "sign on" to the bill, a public declaration that they support the legislative initiative. Co-sponsors are typically solicited at two phases, either prior to its formal introduction, so that the legislation is introduced with strong backing, or after its introduction, to demonstrate growing support for the measure. Obtaining co-sponsors is therefore a crucial tool for park advocates promoting legislation.

For most park-related bills, to move to the congressional hearing phase it is helpful, but not essential, that one or more of the co-sponsors be on the committee that oversees national park matters. In the House of Representatives, the committee with jurisdiction over parks is the Natural Resources Committee (known until recently as the Interior and Insular Affairs Committee), which contains the Subcommittee on National Parks and Public Lands. In the Senate, it is the Energy and Natural Resources Committee and its Subcommittee on Public Lands, National Parks and Forests.

The introduction process itself is very simple. A legislator drafts a bill and "drops it in the hopper" at the desk of the Speaker of the House or the President Pro Tem of the Senate. If you have been in close communication with the legislator's staff regarding the issue, you may have an opportunity to help provide ideas during the drafting phase.

The bill is assigned a number [such as "House Resolution (H.R.) 123" or "Senate Resolution (S.) 123"] and then referred to the appropriate committee for action. It is printed and reproduced, and copies may be obtained through the Senate and House Document rooms. To obtain a bill, write to the Document Room, U.S. House of Representatives, Washington, D.C. 20515 or the Document Room, U.S. Senate, Washington, D.C. 20510.

Copies of the bill also are forwarded to the committee for action. Bills of interest are studied by the members of the committee and their staffs. Achieving a hearing for a bill is the next crucial step. Many factors influence this decision. These include:
- the effectiveness of the bill's sponsor and co-sponsor in securing a commitment from the chair for a hearing
- the interest of the chairman and his/her staff
- the urgency of the subject the bill addresses
- public pressure for action

At times, national park bills "die" in committee, as the hearing calendar may be too full, or the chair of the committee is opposed to the bill and is reluctant to give it a hearing. It may take months, or even several sessions of Congress, for a bill to receive a hearing. In general, bills introduced early in a congressional session, or ones that have strong visible support, have a better chance of receiving a hearing.

Most worthwhile park-related bills receive a public hearing. Hearings are typically conducted in Washington, D.C., but "field hearings" close to the area affected by the bill may also be held. Hearings are conducted to identify the benefits and liabilities of a bill and to identify the extent of support for it. The format may vary, but hearings generally include one or more panels of witnesses, which may include other members of Congress, representatives of the U.S. Department of Interior or the National Park Service, and members of the public. Witnesses are chosen by agreement between the majority and minority members of the subcommittee or committee.

After the hearing is over, the members of Congress and the

committee staff consider the testimony offered and may discuss appropriate revisions to the bill. (The official hearing record is usually left open for about two weeks; during this time written testimony or letters are welcomed. If you are unable to present testimony at a hearing pertaining to your park, you should submit written testimony to the committee, for the record.)

If the subcommittee chair wants to move forward with the legislation, usually within a few weeks after the hearing, the bill is scheduled for a "markup." Many bills receive hearings but experience long delays before markup, while problems and controversies are resolved. Sometimes, if a measure is too controversial or lacks sufficient support, no markup may occur.

During a markup, the revised bill is discussed and voted upon by the subcommittee. Any member of the subcommittee may offer amendments to the bill which may be adopted or rejected. Sometimes a bill is rewritten to such an extent that a substitute bill is offered as an amendment. The subcommittee then votes on whether to send the bill on to the full committee for a subsequent vote. (In the case of the Senate, a bill may be marked up by the full committee directly, rather than going through the subcommittee and then the full committee.)

Once the bill is passed by the full committee, it's referred to the House or Senate floor for a vote. If it's considered noncontroversial, it is typically placed on the Consent Calendar. Legislation on this special calendar must be approved without debate and without objection. If the committee staff has done its work properly, a noncontroversial bill will pass without objection.

If the proposed legislation is controversial, or if a representative objects to the bill, it will be placed on the House Calendar. When the bill is brought up for debate, it is open to amendment.

In theory, a park bill could be filibustered—talking or debating a bill at length in an effort to change it or kill it. This is easier in the Senate, where rules for debate are more relaxed. Senators may also put holds on bills, effectively blocking floor action until their concerns on the park bill or another unrelated bill are addressed. National park bills, however, rarely are subjected to prolonged floor debate to prevent a vote on them. Usually, if a bill is going to be killed, it will die in committee rather than be voted up or down by the full House or Senate.

For a bill to become law, identical bills must pass both houses of Congress. For example, if a bill passes in the House of Representatives, it is sent to the Senate. After Senate hearings, that body may choose to amend the House version before passing the legislation. If the differences are minor, the bill goes back to the House, where that body may concur with the changes. If the differences are major, members of the appropriate committee of each house are appointed to a conference committee to develop a compromise measure.

In reality, very few bills relating to the national parks are conferenced; members and staff of the two committees with jurisdiction usually resolve their differences informally. After there is agreement, the bill is sent back to one or both houses for routine final approval.

Once the House and Senate pass an identical bill, it is sent to the President for signature, at which time it becomes law. A Public Law number is assigned to the new law (such as "PL 102-001"). If the administration disagrees with a bill, the President may veto the measure, although this rarely happens for national park legislation. Once the bill reaches the President, assuming Congress is still in session, he has ten working days to sign or veto it. If he does not act on the bill in that time period, it automatically becomes law.

Because of the large number of parks and public lands bills considered each congressional session, many national park bills are not passed until the very end of each Congress. Because of this, proponents of national park bills must be aware of the possibility of a pocket veto. This legislative strategy is used only on very controversial bills where the administration is opposed to the bill. If Congress passes a bill and then adjourns before the usual ten days have elapsed, and the President fails to sign the bill, it does not become law. The President has "pocketed" the bill.

If legislators are aware of the threat of a veto, they may seek to attach a controversial measure to what they consider a veto-proof bill—a bill the President surely will not veto. That is what happened in 1988 when Manassas National Battlefield Park in

Profile: Amy Meyer

Brooklyn-born Amy Meyer had been amazed by her first glimpse of Yosemite's Tuolumne Meadows when she moved out West. She later explored the Oregon coast, did some kayaking, "learned how to camp," and, as she puts it, got "a taste of how huge the land was—a feeling you don't get in the eastern United States. I was just awed."

Meyer settled in San Francisco in 1958 to raise a family and, in spite of her outdoor adventures and an adopted attachment to the natural beauty of the Bay Area, she still felt somewhat isolated from the world outside her door. Most of her time was committed to raising her two daughters and being involved with her husband's work with the mentally disabled. "I was at a point when I didn't have something very

specific to do. I needed to get involved, to join up with the community—something."

The "something" began to take shape when Meyer showed up at a local Sierra Club meeting in 1970, and eventually led to 23 years of park advocacy, mostly on behalf of the national park she joined the herculean effort to establish—the Golden Gate National Recreation Area (GGNRA). With its 20-million-plus visitors a year, the 75,000-acre GGNRA, a hodgepodge of parklands in San Francisco, Marin and San Mateo counties, is now the most visited national park in the country.

Her life as a park advocate began, of course, with education. Told by a friend early on that an act of Congress was required to establish a national park, Meyer replied matter-of-factly, "Then we'll get an act of Congress," not having the vaguest notion of how to do that.

From the headlands north of Marin to 200-year-old military forts, the previously unprotected parklands in San Francisco were, as Meyer says, "part of the same geological and historical picture, and ought to be understood as a national treasure." Meyer, working out of her Richmond District kitchen as she still does today, co-founded People for a Golden Gate National Recreation Area in 1970 and launched the drive to Washington.

Working together with a small group of volunteers that grew to about 75, the group generated a congressional letter-writing campaign and an impressive coalition of nearly 75 civic and environmental organizations. That was half the battle. The other half lay in persuading two local congressmen—Democrat Phillip Burton and Republican William Mailliard—to take their proposal to Capitol Hill. Burton, Meyer recalls, was "the secret to the whole plan. It was the absolute political genius on his part that made it happen." With Burton leading the bipartisan persuasion in the House, the act passed—unanimously—just two years after Meyer and friends had begun drawing up the plans.

Today the group consists of about 40 civic leaders, from county supervisors to environmental activists and lawyers—and serves as an information network that advises the Park Service on planning and policy. The mimeograph machine and typewriter in Meyer's kitchen which used to churn out postcards and congressional letters have been replaced by a computer and fax, but the workload hasn't changed. The committee is now entrenched in the equally daunting task of converting the famous Army Presidio into national parkland.

"This is a park unlike any other," Meyer says. "It has the highest concentration of historical buildings in the National Park System. But you can't freeze-dry them and make a museum out of them, you have to use them and find a way to make the park pay for itself."

That's one of the challenges ahead for a savvy and seasoned activist like Meyer, now 60, who leads the planning effort and is as comfortable meeting with a member of Congress as one of her many volunteers. "There are always those who have selfish interests in mind and who don't care. But, as I discovered, there's a whole cadre of people out there who *do* care, and who would be on your side if they only knew what your side is!"

Virginia was threatened by the construction of a shopping mall. Toward the end of the congressional session, Congress passed a bill providing for a "legislative taking" of the threatened land and attached it to a tax-reform bill. Although the Manassas bill surely would have been vetoed had it been presented to the President for signature on its own, President Reagan was not willing to veto the major tax-reform bill to which it was attached.

The Appropriations Process

Each year, the President submits a compendium of numbers, charts and complex tables to Congress—the proposed budget of the United States. So massive is this document that its pages are not even comprehensively numbered. Yet, if you look carefully, each year you will find two pages tucked away that outline the proposed budget of the National Park Service.

But by the time the administration submits its budget to Congress, many important decisions regarding spending already have taken place. That is why it is important to know a little about the budget cycle. If you take action at the appropriate time, you do have an opportunity to have an effect on your park's budget.

The Annual Budget Cycle

The time involved from formulating the budget to execution usually is about 18 to 20 months. Because of the long lead time, at any given moment the National Park Service is working concurrently on budgets for three different fiscal years: the year in progress; the upcoming fiscal year for which the budget has been submitted; and the succeeding fiscal year for which budget estimates are being formulated.

Over the course of the budget cycle, many organizations and individuals play key roles. The National Park Service, for example, defines its needs and prepares a budget request that is shaped by the operating requirements of the individual parks and the regional and Washington offices. The operational and political priorities of the Director of the National Park Service, the Assistant Secretary for Fish, Wildlife and Parks, and the Secretary of the Interior also play important roles in influencing the administration's proposed budget.

Around March of each year, the Washington office of the National Park Service issues a budget call. Guidelines are sent to the parks on how to formulate projected budget needs for the fiscal year beginning in October of the next year (about 19 months away). Individual parks and NPS regional offices develop their budget requests and develop proposals for several appropriation accounts: "Operations of the National Park System" (known as "ONPS," this account funds park and regional office operations), "Construction" (money needed for road, trail and facility construction), and "Land Acquisition" (money needed to purchase lands within the park's legislative boundary).

ONPS funds are generally not available to buy land for national parks. Practically all land-acquisition money comes out of a fund set aside for that specific purpose—the Land and Water Conservation Fund. This special Treasury account provides money for federal land acquisition and helps to fund many recreation and land-acquisition programs at the state and local levels. The fund derives its revenue from federal offshore lease fees and royalties and other sources. About $900 million is credited to the fund annually, yet each year less than half that amount is actually appropriated (the balance of unappropriated funds remains unobligated and is used by the President's budget office to help offset the overall budget deficit). Each year, the National Park Service must request LWCF funds from Congress as part of the annual budget cycle in order to have money on hand to buy lands for park purposes.

In January and February, each park sets priorities for its operations, construction and land-acquisition needs, then sends a request to the regional office, which in turn establishes priorities for the region. The regional office then sends these requests to the Washington office. There, the regional budget needs are assessed from a national perspective and sent to the offices of the Assistant Secretary and Interior Secretary, where they are again reviewed and often modified. The proposed budget then is sent to the Office of Management and Budget (OMB), where it is reviewed and usually modified yet again. By the time the administration's budget is presented to Congress in January, some of the priority needs of the individual parks and the Park Service as a whole have been lost in the shuffle.

Usually in February, Congress begins the process of reviewing and revising the budget. Hearings are conducted on the Interior Department budget in the House of Representatives by the House Subcommittee on National Parks and Public Lands, which issues a report with funding level recommendations for the House's budget and appropriations committees to consider. The House Appropriations Subcommittee on Interior conducts its own separate hearings. In the Senate, the Appropriations Subcommittee on Interior and Related Agencies also conducts hearings on the needs of the Park Service.

The House's appropriations subcommittee then marks up the budget bill and sends it to the floor for a vote. After the bill is approved and sent to the Senate, the Senate Appropriations Subcommittee on Interior and Related Agencies marks up its version of the budget and sends it to the Senate floor for a vote. Differences between the House and Senate appropriation bills are "conferenced," or mediated, to resolve differences. Last-minute, behind-the-scenes deals are cut by members of the conference committees, and by September or October, the final budget is routinely approved. By mid-September or October, congressional action on the budget is usually complete and sent to the President for a signature.

How to Influence a Park's Budget

There are basically two opportunities for you as a park advocate to influence the budget process—early in the year when the superintendent of your park is preparing the annual budget request for the fiscal year two years hence, and throughout the year by making your park's needs known to your U.S. representative and senator. Because the typical park superintendent may be reluctant or forbidden to initiate discussions with members of Congress regarding budget needs, *this responsibility falls on you and other park advocates.*

Here are a few pointers for maximizing your effect on the budget for your park:

•**Meet with park staff and find out the real needs of the park.** Learn what the superintendent hopes to accomplish in the next year. Take note of needs, especially for additional personnel, land acquisition and construction. Because the park budget is usually built on last year's "base funding" for the ONPS account, find out what the two or three top priorities are for *new* funding in the next year (perhaps another interpretive ranger position, acquisition of a threatened parcel of land, etc.). If you have specific recommendations about needs, discuss these too with the superintendent. Mutually agree to accomplish a few priority needs and work hard to see them funded rather than spreading your energies and requests too thin with dozens of budget requests.

•**Make an appointment with your representative and/ or senator or their staff.** Spell out the needs of the park. You may want to prepare a one-page fact sheet outlining any budget deficiency and need. If possible, justify the request with facts, statistics and quotes from reliable sources. This fact sheet will serve as the basis for all future correspondence with the representative, senators, or even with the editor of the local paper.

If you don't have the time to meet personally with the representative or senator, write him or her a brief letter outlining your concerns and request a response. In your letter you may want to request that the official contact the chairman of the appropriations subcommittee on Interior to seek the needed funds. If you can get other groups to write or get a number of local organizations to co-sign your letter, you may have more influence with the representative (since, in essence, you are building a local coalition).

•**Try to get the representative personally committed to the park.** The specific influence your representative and senators have on the appropriations process depends on their seniority, what committee assignments they have, who they know well on the appropriations committees, and what their personal interests are. If your representative sits on the appropriations committee, you have a very good opportunity to attain your budget goal. If the representative has not visited the park recently, you may want to host a visit. If you belong to a park support organization, invite the representative to speak at an annual dinner or meeting. Try to build a lasting and personal rapport.

•**Garner as many supporters as possible for the budget item.** Potential supports include chambers of commerce, special visitor groups such as hiking clubs or historical societies, and local landowners.

•**Find out who works on national park issues in your representative's office.** Even though you may not gain direct access to the representative, keep in mind that it usually is the congressional staffer who does most of the work. Brief that individual as well as the local staff assistant on the needs of the park. Get to know them on a first-name basis. If the representative does not seem eager to help, generating a letter-writing campaign may prove fruitful. Politicians respond to public pressure. Individual letters sent by constituents, especially if received in significant numbers, cannot be ignored.

•**Submit written testimony to congressional appropriations committees.** Find out when the hearings are being held from your contact on your representative's staff. Outline the park's needs with as much information as possible. Mail the testimony to: House (Senate) Appropriations Committee, U.S. House of Representatives (Senate), Washington, D.C. 20515 (20510).

By effectively working the appropriations process, you can influence the budget for the park, in some instances even more than the park superintendent can. Only with sufficient staff and monies to operate can we sustain a viable National Park System.

Appendices

• Appendix A •
Additional Resources/Reading Materials

Chapter 2

America's National Parks and Their Keepers, Ronald Foresta, Resources for the Future, Washington, D.C., 1985.

Battling for the National Parks, George B. Hartzog, Jr., Moyer Bell, Ltd., Mount Kisco, NY, 1988.

The Birth of the National Park Service: The Founding Years, 1913-33, Horace M. Albright and Robert Cahn, Howe Brothers, Salt Lake City, 1985.

National Park Service: The Story Behind the Scenery, Horace M. Albright with Russell E. Dickenson and William Penn Mott, Jr., K.C. Publications, Las Vegas, 1987.

National Parks: The American Experience, Alfred Runte, University of Nebraska Press, Lincoln, 1987 (revised).

National Parks for a New Generation, Conservation Foundation, Washington, D.C., 1985.

National Parks: From Vignettes to a Global View, Commission on Research and Resource Management Policy in the National Park System, National Parks and Conservation Association, 1989.

The National Parks: Index, National Park Service, Washington, D.C., 1991.

The National Parks: Shaping the System, National Park Service, 1991.

Preserving Different Pasts: The American Natural Monuments, Hall Rothman, University of Illinois Press, Urbana, 1989.

"Recommended Readings on the National Park Service: Its History and Mission," National Parks and Conservation Association, 1992.

Regreening the National Parks, Michael Frome, University of Arizona Press, Tucson, 1991.

Steve Mather of the National Parks, Alfred Shankland, Alfred A. Knopf, New York, 1976.

Chapter 3

Organizing: A Guide for Grassroots Leaders, Si Kahn, McGraw-Hill, New York, 1982.

Organizing for Social Change: A Manual for Activists in the '90's, Kim Bobo, Jackie Kendall, Steve Max, Seven Locks Press, Cabin John, Maryland, 1991.

Chapter 4

Bacon's Newspaper Directory, Bacon's Information, Inc., Chicago, IL, published annually.

Bacon's TV/Radio Directory, Bacon's Information, Inc., Chicago, IL, published annually.

Bacon's Magazine Directory, Bacon's Information, Inc., Chicago, IL, published annually.

Chapter 5

"Adjacent Land Use and National Parks," Conservation Foundation, 1990.

Case Studies in Protecting Parks, National Park Service, U.S. Natural Resources Report 87-2 (December 1987).

Creating Successful Communities: A Guidebook to Growth Management Strategies, Conservation Foundation, 1990.

"External Development Affecting the National Parks," University of Colorado School of Law, Natural Resources Law Center conference proceedings, 1986.

"Helpless Giants: The National Parks and the Regulation of Private Lands," Joseph L. Sax, *Michigan Law Review* 239, 1976.

Islands Under Siege: National Parks and the Politics of External Threats, John C. Freemuth, University of Kansas Press, Lawrence, 1991.

"Limited Progress Made in Documenting and Mitigating Threats to the Parks," General Accounting Office, 1987.

Managing National Park System Resources: A Handbook on Legal Duties, Opportunities and Tools, Michael A. Mantell, editor, The Conservation Foundation, Washington, D.C, 1990.

"On Protecting the National Parks From the External Threats Dilemma," Robert B. Keiter, *Land and Water Law Review*, Vol. 20, pg. 355, 1985.

Our Common Lands: Defending the National Parks, David J. Simon, editor, National Parks and Conservation Association, Washington, D.C., 1988.

Chapter 6

NPS-2, NPS Planning Process—available from any NPS regional office.

Nature Resources: Island Theory and Conservation Practice, Craig L. Shafer, Smithsonian Institution Press, Washington, D.C. 1990.

Chapter 7

The following organizations specialize in land acquisition to benefit national parks and other important public lands. In addition, draw on the resources and support of local land trusts.

National Park Trust
P.O. Box 40236
Washington, D.C. 20016
(202) 625-2268

The Nature Conservancy
1815 North Lynn Street
Arlington, VA 22209
(703) 841-5300

The Trust for Public Land
116 New Montgomery - 4th Floor
San Francisco, CA 94105
(415) 495-4014

Chapter 8

Visitor Impact Management: A Review of Research, and *Visitor Impact Management: The Planning Framework*, Alan R. Graefe, Fred R. Kuss and Jerry Vaske, National Parks and Conservation Association, Washington, D.C., 1990.

Carrying Capacity in the National Parks, Robert Manning, report for the National Park Service, Washington, D.C.

Wilderness Management, John C. Hendee, George H. Stankey and Robert

C. Lucas, North American Press, Golden, Colorado, 1990.

Wildland Recreation, William E. Hammitt and David N. Cole, John S. Wiley & Sons, New York, 1987.

Chapter 9

Conserving Rivers: A Handbook for State Action, Kevin J. Coyle and Christopher N. Brown, National Park Service, 1992.

Park Waters in Peril, National Parks and Conservation Association, 1993.

Rivers at Risk: The Concerned Citizen's Guide to Hydropower, John D. Echeverria, Pope Barrow, and Richard Roos-Collins, Island Press, 1989.

Chapter 10

"A Citizen's Guide to Clean Air," Conservation Foundation, 1972.

Clean Air Act of 1970—Citizen Enforcement, Richard Ayres, Natural Resources Defense Council, 1970.

Community Air Quality Planning Handbook, Environmental Law Institute, 1979.

"Clean Air. It's Up to You, Too," Environmental Protection Agency, 1973.

Chapter 11

All of these documents should be available from any National Park Service regional office:

Management Policies, Department of Interior, National Park Service, 1988

Planning Process Guideline (NPS-2)

NEPA Compliance Guideline (NPS-12)

Cultural Resource Management Guideline (NPS-28)

Natural Resource Management Guideline (NPS-77)

NPS Interpretive Planning Handbook, 1983

Chapter 12

Our Common Lands, David J. Simon, editor, National Parks and Conservation Association, Washington, D.C., 1988.

Managing National Park System Resources: A Handbook on Legal Duties, Opportunities and Tools, Michael A. Mantell, editor, The Conservation Foundation, Washington, D.C., 1990.

Chapter 13

The Environmental Impact Statement Process—A Guide to Citizen Action, Information Resources Press, 1978.

Our Common Lands, David J. Simon, editor, National Parks and Conservation Association, 1988.

Chapter 14

The Almanac of American Politics. Issued annually by National Journal, 1730 M Street, N.W., Washington, D.C. 20036.

Congressional Directory. Issued each Congress by U.S. Government Printing Office, Washington, D.C. 20402.

Politics in America. Issued each Congress by Congressional Quarterly, Inc., 1414 22nd Street, N.W., Washington, D.C. 20037.

• Appendix B •
National Parks and Conservation Association at a Glance

•Membership: 400,000
•Staff: 56
•Percentage of Donations Devoted to Programs: 75.2%

National Headquarters:
National Parks and Conservation Association
1776 Massachusetts Avenue, N.W.
Washington, D.C. 20036
Toll-free (800) NAT-PARK or (202) 223-6722

Conservation Policy	ext. 231
Development	ext. 130
Editorial (*National Parks* magazine)	ext. 200
Grassroots Programs	ext. 220
Marketing	ext. 140
Membership	ext. 213
Public Affairs	ext. 121

Regional Offices (see pages 213-214 for addresses):

Alaska Region (Anchorage, AK): (907) 277-6722
    Chip Dennerlein, Regional Director
Heartland Region (Woodbury, MN): (612) 735-8008
    Lori Nelson, Regional Director
Northeast Region (Washington, D.C.): (202) 223-6722
    Bruce Craig, Regional Director
Pacific Northwest Region (Seattle, WA): (206) 824-8808
    Dale Crane, Regional Director
Southwest Region (Albuquerque, NM): (505) 247-1221
    Dave Simon, Regional Director
Rocky Mountain Region (Salt Lake City, UT): (801) 532-4796
    Terri Martin, Regional Director
Southeast Region (Norris, TN): (615) 494-9786
    Don Barger, Regional Director

NPCA Programs and Services

Founded in 1919, the National Parks and Conservation Association (NPCA) is America's only private nonprofit citizens organization dedicated solely to protecting, enhancing and promoting public understanding of the National Park System. With a membership of more than 400,000, NPCA accomplishes its mission through activities on the national, regional, state and grassroots levels. Programs include:

•**Park Activist Network**: NPCA's park activist network is made up of park activists and ParkWatchers. This grassroots program alerts members to severe threats facing the parks, immediately mobilizing those members to action. Park activists write letters encouraging opinion leaders to protect our national parks. ParkWatchers provide NPCA's staff with critical information from all over the country about new and continued threats to specific parks.

•**National Park Advocacy**: NPCA works at the national, regional and grassroots levels to address a wide variety of environmental and other issues affecting existing national parks, as well as working to expand the National Park System to protect the most significant of America's historic, cultural and ecological areas.

•**Regional Advocacy**: To address regional park issues and encourage grassroots action on behalf of the parks, NPCA staffs seven field offices in the Pacific Northwest, Southwest, Rocky Mountain, Heartland, Southeast, Northeast, and Alaska regions.

•**Congressional Initiatives**: NPCA experts consult with members of Congress and representatives of various federal agencies on laws and regulations to protect and enhance the national parks. In addition, NPCA is often called upon to testify at congressional hearings and help formulate park protection legislation. NPCA also works to ensure protection of parklands at the local, state and regional levels.

•**Publications**: NPCA publishes *National Parks,* an award-winning magazine covering the most important issues facing national parks. The bimonthly magazine reaches more than 400,000 people. NPCA also produces The *ParkWatcher*, a bimonthly newsletter on regional issues requiring grassroots citizen action.

•**March for Parks**: The nation's first and largest walk event for parks and open spaces, March for Parks is held each year in conjunction with Earth Day. With support from national corporations and local businesses, hundreds of marches in all 50 states are planned by environmental and conservation associations, hiking and walking groups, schools, youth and service clubs, and individuals. These events raise money for park improvement, protection, and education projects benefiting local, state, regional and national parks.

•**Corporate Partnerships**: NPCA realizes the important role of business in the conservation of our national parks. NPCA's marketing program, which encompasses licensing, sponsorship and cause-related marketing, provides corporations with numerous opportunities to make a positive impact in the parks.

•A toll-free **National Park Information Hotline** provides NPCA members with information about national parks and member services.

Recent NPCA Accomplishments

•Periodically, NPCA releases reports on the parks providing in-depth analysis of the major threats facing our national parks. ***Parks In Peril: The Race Against Time Continues,*** was published in 1992. This report draws substantial media and public attention to park issues. Newspaper coverage alone reached more than 80 million readers in 1992.

•In the past two years, NPCA efforts have contributed to the addition of several new units to the National Park System: Salt River Bay National Historical Park and Ecological Preserve in the U.S. Virgin Islands; Mary McLeod Bethune Council House in Washington, D.C.; Manzanar National Historic Site in California; Niobrara National Scenic and Recreational River in Nebraska; and Dry Tortugas National Park in the Florida Keys.

•Successful efforts to preserve America's Civil War heritage include NPCA's significant role in the expansion of Gettysburg National Military Park, NPCA's active participation in the national fight to save a portion of the Manassas battlefield from shopping mall development, and the publication in 1992 of the brochure, *Visiting Battlefields: The Civil War.*

•*The National Park System Plan: A Blueprint for Tomorrow* was published by NPCA in 1988 as the first comprehensive action plan for the future of the parks. Its nine volumes include more than 150 major recommendations for improvement of the National Park System in the areas of resource protection, research, visitation, interpretation, planning and land acquisition. Implementation of these recommendations is the focus of many of NPCA's efforts.

•NPCA has developed a number of programs to reintroduce endangered species and replant native vegetation in national parks throughout the country. These efforts have led to the planting of more than 40,000 redwood saplings in Redwood National Park in California, and to a partnership for the reintroduction of the endangered red wolf in Great Smoky Mountains National Park.

•NPCA published the *Visitor Impact Management Study,* a first-of-its-kind tool for evaluating the effects of the more than 274 million people who visit America's national parks each year.

•Through its national media campaign, NPCA works to increase public awareness of the need to reform federal laws governing national park concessions. Editorials on the subject have appeared in many papers, including the *New York Times, Denver Post, New Orleans Times-Picayune, Portland Oregonian,* and the *Birmingham (AL) News.*

•In 1991, NPCA launched its **Save Our National Parks Campaign** to encourage citizen involvement in park protection and preservation issues and activities. The annual March for Parks is the centerpiece of this citizen action campaign.

•1993 saw the inauguration of a new corporate partnership project, the **National Park Restoration Partners Program**, geared to involving businesses and corporations as partners in NPCA programs to protect and improve the nation's national parks.

• Appendix C •
Park Advocacy and Friends Groups

Each group is listed under the name of the park or parks with which it is associated. *This is only a partial list.* If you do not find the national park nearest you listed, contact your park for the names of groups in your area. Parks identified as "NCR" are part of the National Capital Region.

ALABAMA
LITTLE RIVER CANYON NATIONAL
PRESERVE
Friends of the Little River Canyon
P.O. Box 111
Mentone, AL 35984

ALASKA
DENALI NATIONAL PARK AND
PRESERVE
Denali Citizen Council
P.O. Box 78
Denali Park, AK 99755

GLACIER BAY NATIONAL PARK AND
PRESERVE
Friends of Glacier Bay
P.O. Box 135
Gustavus, AK 99826

WRANGELL-ST. ELIAS NATIONAL PARK
AND PRESERVE
Friends of Kennicott
3018 Alder Circle
Anchorage, AK 99508

ARIZONA
GRAND CANYON NATIONAL PARK
Grand Canyon Trust
Route 4, Box 718
Flagstaff, AZ 86001

HUBBELL TRADING POST NATIONAL
HISTORIC SITE
Friends of Hubbell Trading Post NHS
P.O. Box 1380
Ganado, AZ 85717

TUMACACORI NATIONAL MONUMENT
Los Amigos de Tumacacori
P.O. Box 67
Tumacacori, AZ 85640

WALNUT CANYON
NATIONAL MONUMENT
Friends of Walnut Canyon
P.O. Box 835
Flagstaff, AZ 86004

ARKANSAS
FORT SMITH NATIONAL HISTORIC
SITE
Old Fort Militia
P.O. Box 517
Fort Smith, AR 72902

HOT SPRINGS NATIONAL PARK
Friends of the Fordyce & Hot Springs
National Park
P.O. Box 172
Hot Springs NP, AR 719032

OZARK NATIONAL SCENIC RIVERWAYS
The Ozark Society, Inc.
P.O. Box 2914
Little Rock, Arkansas 72203

CALIFORNIA
CHANNEL ISLANDS NATIONAL PARK
Friends of Channel Islands National Park
1901 Spinnaker Drive
Ventura, CA 93001

DEATH VALLEY NATIONAL MONUMENT
Death Valley 49ers, Inc.
Box 338
Death Balley, CA 92328

EUGENE O'NEILL NATIONAL
HISTORIC SITE
Eugene O'Neill Foundation
P.O. Box 402
Danville, CA 94526

FORT POINT NATIONAL
HISTORIC SITE
Friends of Fort Point National Historic Site
P.O. Box 29333
San Francisco, CA 94129

GOLDEN GATE NATIONAL
RECREATION AREA
Fort Mason Foundation
Fort Mason Center
San Francisco, CA 94123

People for a Golden Gate NRA
3627 Clement Street
San Francisco, CA 94121

JOHN MUIR NATIONAL HISTORIC SITE
John Muir Memorial Association
P.O. Box 2433
Martinez, CA 94553

LASSEN VOLCANIC NATIONAL PARK
Lassen Volcanic National Park
Foundation
P.O. Box 8
Mineral, CA 95928

PINNACLES NATIONAL MONUMENT
Friends of Pinnacles
122 Parnell Street
Santa Cruz, CA 95062

SANTA MONICA MOUNTAINS
NATIONAL RECREATION AREA
Allied Artists of the Santa Monica
Mountains
17741 Nordhoff Street
Northbridge, CA 91325

Friends of Satwiwa
4126 Potrero Road
Newbury Park, CA 91320

Mountains Conservancy Foundation
3800 Solstice Canyon Road
Malibu, CA 90265

Santa Monica Parkland Association
30401 Agoura Road 100
Agoura Hills, CA 91301

SEQUOIA NATIONAL PARK
KINGS CANYON NATIONAL PARK
Sequoia & Kings Cayon National Parks
Foundation
Ash Mountain, Box 10
Three Rivers, CA 93271

YOSEMITE NATIONAL PARK
Yosemite Fund
155 Montgomery Street 1104
San Francisco, CA 34104

COLORADO
FLORISSANT FOSSIL BEDS NATIONAL
MONUMENT
Friends of the Fossil Beds
P.O. Box 394
Florissant, CO 80816

GREAT SAND DUNES NATIONAL
MONUMENT
Friends of the Dunes, Inc.
11500 Highway 150
Mosca, CO 81146

MESA VERDE NATIONAL PARK
Friends of Mesa Verde
P.O. Drawer 1750
Cortez, CO 81321

ROCKY MOUNTAIN NATIONAL PARK
Rocky Mountain National Park
Associates, Inc.
Rocky Mountain National Park
Estes Park, CO 80517

CONNECTICUT
WEIR FARM NATIONAL HISTORIC SITE
Weir Farm Heritage Trust
735 Nod Hill Road
Wilton, CT 06897

DISTRICT OF COLUMBIA
BATTERY KEMBLE PARK (NCR)
Friends of Battery Kemble Park
2832 Chain Bridge Road, N.W.
Washington, DC 20016-3406

MERIDIAN HILL PARK (NCR)
Friends of Meridian Hill, Inc.
2120 16th Street, N.W.
Washington, DC 20009

MONTROSE PARK (NCR)
Friends of Montrose Park
3022 Q Street, N.W.
Washington, DC 20007

SHENANDOAH NATIONAL PARK
Shenandoah National Park Coalition
1776 Massachusetts Avenue, N.W.
Washington, DC 20036

FLORIDA
BIG CYPRESS NATIONAL PRESERVE
Big Cypress Recreation Association
HCR Box 110
Ochopee, FL 33943

CANAVERAL NATIONAL SEASHORE
Friends of Canaveral National Seashore
P.O. Box 1526
New Smyrna Beach, FL 32170

Space Coast Friends of Canaveral
National Seashore Park
750 Country Club Drive
Titusville, FL 32780

EVERGLADES NATIONAL PARK
Friends of the Everglades
101 Westward Drive #2
Miami Springs, FL 33166

GEORGIA
ANDERSONVILLE NATIONAL
HISTORIC SITE
Friends of Andersonville
Route 1, Box 800
Andersonville, GA 31711

KENNESAW MOUNTAIN NATIONAL
BATTLEFIED PARK
Friends of Kennesaw Mountain National
Battlefied Park
900 Kennesaw Mountain Drive
Kennesaw, GA 30144

HAWAII
KALAUPAPA NATIONAL
HISTORICAL PARK
Friends of Father Damien
P.O. Box 6016
Honolulu, HI 96818

PU'UHONUA O HONAUNAU NATIONAL
HISTORICAL PARK
Kahua Na'au A'o Ma Pu'Uhonua O
Honaunau
P.O. Box 788
Honaunau, Kona HI 96726-0788

PUUKOHOLA HEIAU NATIONAL
HISTORIC SITE
Na Aikane O Puukohola Heiau
78-6831 Alii Drive 232
Kailua-Kona, HI 96740

Na Koe O Puukohola
P.O. Box 44340
Kawaihae, HI 96743

IDAHO
CITY OF ROCKS NATIONAL RESERVE
Friends of City of Rocks, Inc.
P.O. Box 2053
Idaho Falls, ID 83403

CRATERS OF THE MOON NATIONAL
MONUMENT
The Craters of the Moon Project
P.O. Box 4715
Boise, ID 83711

HAGERMAN FOSSIL BEDS NATIONAL
MONUMENT
Hagerman Fossil Council, Inc.
Box 488
Hagerman, ID 83332

INDIANA
INDIANA DUNES NATIONAL
LAKESHORE
Friends of Indiana Dunes
P.O. Box 166
Beverly Shores, IN 46301

Save the Dunes Council
444 Barker Road
Michigan City, IN 46460

KANSAS
FORT LARNED NATIONAL
HISTORIC SITE
Fort Larned Old Guard, Inc.
Fort Larned NHS
Larned, KS 67550

KENTUCKY
CUMBERLAND GAP NATIONAL
HISTORICAL PARK
Cumberland Gap Historic Foundation
414 Fayette Place
Lexington, KY 40508

MAMMOTH CAVE NATIONAL PARK
Mammoth Cave National Park
Association
Mammoth Cave, KY 42259

MAINE
ACADIA NATIONAL PARK
Friends of Acadia
P.O. Box 725
Bar Harbor, ME 04609

MARYLAND
ANTIETAM NATIONAL BATTLEFIELD
Save Historic Antietam Foundation, Inc.
P.O. Box 550
Sharpsburg, MD 21782

ASSATEAGUE ISLAND NATIONAL
SEASHORE
Committee to Preserve Assateague
Island, Inc.
105 West Chesapeake Avenue 413
Baltimore, MD 21204-4739

CATOCTIN MOUNTAIN PARK (NCR)
Friends of Big Hunting Creek
7003 Glen Court
Frederick, MD 21702

CHESAPEAKE AND OHIO CANAL
NATIONAL HISTORICAL PARK
Chesapeake & Ohio Canal
Association, Inc.
OP.O. Box 366
Glen Echo, MD 20812

Friends of Great Falls Tavern
11725 Piney Meeting House Road
Potomac, MD 20854

FORT McHENRY NATIONAL
MONUMENT AND HISTORIC SHRINE
Patriots of Fort McHenry
Fort McHenry National Shrine
Baltimore, MD 21230

FRIENDSHIP HILL NATIONAL
HISTORIC SITE
Friendship Hill Association
7300 Macarthur Blvd.
Glen Echo, MD 20812

GLEN ECHO PARK (NCR)
The Glen Echo Park Foundation
7300 Macarthur Blvd.
Glen Echo, MD 20812

MONACACY NATIONAL BATTLEFIELD
Friends of Monacacy Battlefield, Inc.
P.O. Box 4101
Frederick, MD 21705-4101

MASSACHUSETTS
ADAMS NATIONAL HISTORIC SITE
Quincy Partnership
P.O. Box 488
Qunicy, MA 02170

BOSTON NATIONAL
HISTORICAL PARK
Freedom Trail Foundation
Charlestown Navy Yard
Boston, MA 02129

CAPE COD NATIONAL SEASHORE
Friends of the Cape Cod
National Seashore, Inc.
Box 550
Wellfleet, MA 02667

LOWELL NATIONAL HISTORICAL PARK
Lowell Regatta Festival Foundation
P.O. Box 217
Lowell, MA 01853

MINUTEMAN NATIONAL
HISTORICAL PARK
The Friends of Battle Road
P.O. Box 95
Lincoln Center, MA 01973

SALEM MARITIME NATIONAL
HISTORIC SITE
The Salem Partnership
6 Central Street
Salem, MA 01970

SPRINGFIELD ARMORY NATIONAL
HISTORIC SITE
Springfield Central
338 Worthington Street
Springfield, MA 01103

MICHIGAN
SLEEPING BEAR DUNES NATIONAL
LAKESHORE
The Leelanau Conservancy
105 N. 1st St.
P.O. Box 1007
Leland, MI 49654

MINNESOTA
GRAND PORTAGE
NATIONAL MONUMENT
Friends of Grand Portage
506 West Michigan Street
Duluth, MN 55802

MISSISSIPPI NATIONAL RIVER AND
RECREATION AREA
Friends of the Mississippi River
26 E. Eschange Street, #215
St. Paul, MN 55101

PIPESTONE NATIONAL MONUMENT
Pipestone County Historical Society
113 S. Hiawatha
Pipestone, MN 56164

VOYAGEURS NATIONAL PARK
Voyageurs Region National
Park Association
119 North 4th Street 302C
Minneapolis, MN 55401

MISSISSIPPI
GULF ISLANDS NATIONAL SEASHORE
Gulf Islands Conservancy
PO Box 1467
Gulfport, MS 39502

NATCHEZ TRACE PARKWAY
Natchez Trace Parkway Association
P.O. Box Drawer A
Tupelo, MS 38802-1210

MISSOURI
OZARK NATIONAL SCENIC
RIVERWAYS
Ozark Heritage Foundation
P.O. Box 490
Van Buren, MO 63965

WILSON'S CREEK
NATIONAL BATTLEFIELD
Wilson's Creek National Battlefield
Foundation
1845 South National Avenue
Springfield, MO 65804

MONTANA
GLACIER NATIONAL PARK
Glacier National Park Associates
P.O. Box 91
Kalispell, MT 59903

LITTLE BIGHORN BATTLEFIELD
NATIONAL MONUMENT
Little Bighorn Preservation Committee
P.O. Box 7
Hardin, MT 59034

YELLOWSTONE NATIONAL PARK
Greater Yellowstone Coalition
P.O. Box 1871
Bozeman, MT 59771

NEBRASKA
AGATE FOSSIL BEDS NATIONAL
MONUMENT
Friends of Agate Fossil Beds, Inc.
P.O. Box 27
Gering, NE 69341

NEVADA
LAKE MEAD NATIONAL
RECREATION AREA
Community Action for
Lake Mead & Mohave
2525 Pinto Lane
Las Vegas, NV 89107

NEW HAMPSIRE
SAINT-GAUDENS NATIONAL
HISTORIC SITE
The Augustus Saint-Gaudens Memorial
RR #3, Box 73
Cornish, NH 03745

NEW JERSEY
EDISON NATIONAL HISTORIC SITE
Friends of Edison National Historic Site
342 Main Street
West Orange, NJ 07052

MORRISTOWN NATIONAL
HISTORICAL PARK
Washington Association of New Jersey
P.O. Box 1473
Morristown, NJ 07960

NEW MEXICO
BANDELIER NATIONAL MONUMENT
Friends of Bandelier
P.O. Box 1282
Los Alamos, NM 87544

EL MALPAIS NATIONAL MONUMENT
Los Amigos Del Malpais
P.O. Box 2336
Milan, NM 87021

PETROGLYPH NATIONAL MONUMENT
Friends of the Alburquerque Petroglyphs
2920 Carlisle NE
Albuquerque, NM 87110

NEW YORK
ELEANOR ROOSEVELT NATIONAL HIS-
TORIC SITE
Eleanor Roosevelt Center At Valkill, Inc.
P.O. Box 255
Hyde Park, NY 12538

FEDERAL HALL NATIONAL MEMORIAL
Society of the National Shrine of the
Bill of Rights
897 South Columbus Avenue
Mount Vernon, NY 10550

FIRE ISLAND NATIONAL SEASHORE
Fire Island Lighthouse Pres. Society, Inc.
Captree Island, P.O. Box 8
Babylon, NY 11702

Fire Island Wilderness Committee
325 Beavertown Road
Brookhaven, NY 11719

FORT STANWIX NATIONAL
MONUMENT
Fort Stanwix Garrison
112 East Park Street
Rome, NY 137440

FREDERICK DOUGLASS NATIONAL
HISTORIC SITE (NCR)
Friends of Frederick Douglass, Inc.
253 West Avenue
Rochester, NY 14611

GATEWAY NATIONAL
RECREATION AREA
Friends of Gateway
72 Reade Street
New York, NY 10007

MARTIN VAN BUREN
NATIONAL HISTORIC SITE
Friends of Lindenwald
P.O. Box 545
Kinderhook, NY 02106

SAINT-GAUDENS
NATIONAL HISTORIC SITE
Saint-Gaudens Memorial
17 East 47th Street
New York, NY 10017

SARATOGA NATIONAL HISTORICAL
PARK
Friends of Saratoga Battlefield
648 Route 32
Stillwater, NY 12170

STATUE OF LIBERTY
NATIONAL MONUMENT
Statue of Liberty-Ellis Island Foundation
52 Vanderbilt Avenue
New York, NY 10017

THEODORE ROOSEVELT INAUGURAL
NATIONAL HISTORIC SITE
Rough Riders/Theodore Roosevelt
Inaugural Site Foundation
641 Delaware
Buffalo, NY 14202

UPPER DELAWARE SCENIC AND
RECREATIONAL RIVER
Friends of the Roebling Bridge
Box 100
Barryville, NY 12719

VANDERBILT MANSION NATIONAL
HISTORIC SITE
Frederick W. Vanderbilt
Garden Assocation Inc.
P.O. Box 239
Hyde Park, NY 12538

Friends of the Power House
P.O. Box 5006
Poughkeepsie, NY 12602

WOMEN'S RIGHTS NATIONAL
HISTORICAL PARK
Elizabeth Cady Stanton Foundation
P.O. Box 603
Seneca Falls, NY 131148

NORTH CAROLINA
BLUE RIDGE PARKWAY
Friends of the Blue Ridge Parkway
P.O. Box 341
Arden, NC 28704

CARL SANDBURG HOME
NATIONAL HISTORIC SITE
The Friends of Connemara
P.O. Box 16
Flat Rock, NC 28731

MOORES CREEK
NATIONAL BATTLEFIELD
Moores Creek Battleground Association
P.O. Box 69
Currie, NC 28435

WRIGHT BROTHERS
NATIONAL MEMORIAL
First Flight Society
P.O. Box 1903
Kitty Hawk, NC 27949

NORTH DAKOTA
FORT UNION TRADING POST
NATIONAL HISTORIC SITE
Friends of Fort Union Trading Post
Fort Union NHS, Bedford Route
Williston, ND 58801

KNIFE RIVER INDIAN VILLAGES
NATIONAL HISTORIC SITE
Knife River Heritage Foundation
P.O. Box 284
Stanton, ND 58571

OHIO
CUYAHOGA VALLEY NATIONAL
RECREATION AREA
Cuyahoga Valley Association
P.O. Box 222
Peninsula, OH 44264

GETTYSBURG NATIONAL
MILITARY PARK
Friends of the National Parks
at Gettysburg
10549 Reading Road
Cincinnati, OH 45241

PERRY'S VICTORY AND INTERNA-
TIONAL PEACE MEMORIAL
The Perry Group
P.O. Box 484
Put-in-Bay, OH 43456

WILLIAM HOWARD TAFT NATIONAL
HISTORIC SITE
Friends of the William Howard Taft
Birthplace
2058 Auburn Avenue # 1
CIncinnati, OH 45219-3050

OKLAHOMA
CHICKASAW NATIONAL
RECREATION AREA
Chickasaw NRA Park Support Committee
113 West Muskogee
Sulphur, OK 73086

OREGON
FORT CLATSOP NATIONAL MEMORIAL
Fort Clatsop Historical Society
Route 3, Box 604-FC
Astoria, OR 97103

Friends of the Columbia River Gorge
519 SW 3rd Avenue
P.O. Box 810
Portland, OR 97240

PENNSYLVANIA
DELAWARE WATER GAP NATIONAL
RECREATION AREA
Pocono Enveronmental Education Center
RD, 2 Box 1016
Dingman's Ferry, PA 18328

GETTYSBURG NATIONAL
MILITARY PARK
Friends of the National Parks
at Gettysburg
P.O. Box 1863
Gettysburg, PA 17325

INDEPENDENCE NATIONAL
HISTORICAL PARK
Friends of Independence
National Historical Park
313 Walnut Street
Philadephia, PA 19106

Independence Hall Preservation Fund
313 Walnut Street
Philadelphia, PA 19106

Independence Hall Association
320 Chestnut Street
Philadelphia, PA 19106

STEAMTOWN NATIONAL
HISTORIC SITE
Friends of Steamtown
160 Andover
Wilkes-Barre, PA 18782

Steamtown Advisory Council
Forum Building 313
Harrisburg, PA 17120

VALLEY FORGE NATIONAL
HISTORICAL PARK
Friends of Valley Forge
P.O. Box 953
Valley Forge, PA 19481

RHODE ISLAND
BLACKSTONE RIVER VALLEY
NATIONAL HERITAGE CORRIDOR
Friends of the Blackstone
6 Vallley Stream Drive
Cumberland, RI 02864

SOUTH CAROLINA
FORT SUMTER NATIONAL MONUMENT
Friends of Historic Snee Farm
P.O. Box 507
Charleston, SC 29402

SOUTH DAKOTA
MOUNT RUSHMORE
NATIONAL MEMORIAL
Mount Rushmore National
Memorial Society
P.O. Box 1066
Rapid City, SD 57709

Citizens Protecting Mt. Rushmore
P.O. Box 706
Keystone, SD 57751

TENNESSEE
CHICKAMAUGA & CHATTANOOGA
NATIONAL MILITARY PARK
Friends of Chickamauga & Chattanooga
National Military Park
P.O. Box 748
Chattanooga, TN 37401

GREAT SMOKY MOUNTAINS
NATIONAL PARK
Friends of the Great Smoky Mountains
1508 Monterey Avenue
Kingsport, TN 37664

Foothills Parkway Association
P.O. Box 4516
Sevierville, TN 37864-4516

OBED WILD AND SCENIC RIVER
Tennessee Citizens for
Wilderness Planning
130 Tabor Road
Oak Ridge, TN 37830

SHILOH NATIONAL MILITARY PARK
Friends of Shiloh
P.O. Box 100
Shiloh, TN 38376

STONES RIVER
NATIONAL BATTLEFIELD
Friends of the Stones River
National Battlefield
P.O. Box 4092
Murfresboro, TN 37122-4092

TEXAS
AMISTAD NATIONAL
RECREATION AREA
Friends of Amistad
P.O. Box 420367
Del Rio, TX 78842-0367

LYNDON B. JOHNSON NATIONAL
HISTORICAL PARK
L.B.J. Heartland Council
HC 13, Box 4
Fredericksburg, TX 78624

SAN ANTONIO MISSIONS
NATIONAL HISTORICAL PARK
Los Compadres de San Antonio Missions
National Historical Park
6539 San Jose Drive
San Antonio, TX 78214

UTAH
CANYONLANDS NATIONAL PARK
Canyonlands Field Institute
P.O. Box 68
Moab, UT 84532

GOLDEN SPIKE
NATIONAL HISTORIC SITE
Golden Spike Association of
Box Elder County
106 West 100 North
Brigham City, UT 84302

VERMONT
MARSH-BILLINGS NATIONAL
HISTORICAL PARK
Billings Farm Museum/Woodstock
Foundation, Inc.
P.O. Box 489
Woodstock, VT 05091

VIRGIN ISLANDS (U.S.)
VIRGIN ISLANDS NATIONAL PARK
Friends of the Virgin Islands National Park
P.O. Box 8317
St. John, VI 00831

St. Croix Environmental Association
Christiansted
St. Croix, VI 00822

VIRGINIA
CLAUDE MOORE COLONIAL FARM AT
TURKEY RUN (NCR)
Farm Family Members
9310 Georgetown Pike
McLean, VA 22101

Friends of the Claude Moore
Colonial Farm
6310 Georgetown Pike
McLean, VA 22101

COLONIAL NATIONAL
HISTORICAL PARK
Yorktown Day Association
P.O. Box 210
Yorktown, VA 23690

GEORGE WASHINGTON MEMORIAL
PARKWAY (NCR)
The Friends of Dyke Marsh, Inc.
7212 Beechwood Drive
Alexandria, VA 22307

GREEN SPRINGS HISTORIC DISTRICT
The Historic Green Springs, Inc.
P.O. Box 1685
Louisa, VA 23093

MAGGIE L. WALKER NATIONAL
HISTORIC SITE
Maggie L. Walker Historical Foundation
P.O. Box 26078
Richmond, VA 23261

MANASSAS NATIONAL
BATTLEFIELD PARK
Save the Battlefield Coalition
P.O. Box 14
Catharpin, VA 22018

PETERSBURG NATIONAL
BATTLEFIELD/APPOMATTOX COURT
HOUSE NATIONAL
HISTORICAL PARK
Friends of Virginia Civil War Parks, Inc.
1708 Hickory Hill Road
Petersburg, VA 23804

PRINCE WILLIAM FOREST PARK
Friends of Prince William Forest Park
P.O. Box 209
Triangle, VA 22172

SHENANDOAH NATIONAL PARK
Piedmont Environmental Council
P.O. Box 460
Warrenton, VA 22186

WASHINGTON
COULEE DAM NATIONAL
RECREATION AREA
Camp NA-BOR-LEE Association
113 West Muskogee
Davenport, WA 99122

FORT VANCOUVER NATIONAL
HISTORIC SITE
Friends of Fort Vancouver National
Historic Site
612 East Reserve Street
Vancouver, WA 58801

MOUNT RAINIER NATIONAL PARK
Mount Rainier National Park Associates
5325 Montas Vista Drive East
Sumner, WA 98390

NORTH CASCADES NATIONAL PARK
North Cascades Conservation Council
P.O. Box 95980, Univ. Station
Seattle, WA 89145-1980

OLYMPIC NATIONAL PARK
Olympic Park Assiciation
13245 40th,, NE
Seattle, WA 98124

Save Our Shoreline
Route,1, Box 716
Davenport, WA 99122

WEST VIRGINIA
HARPERS FERRY NATIONAL
HISTORICAL PARK
Friends of Harpers Ferry National Park
Route 3, Box 98
Harpers Ferry, WV 25425

WISCONSIN
ST. CROIX NATIONAL SCENIC
RIVERWAY
St. Croix River Association
P.O. Box 705
Hudson, WI 54016

WYOMING
GRAND TETON NATIONAL PARK
YELLOWSTONE NATIONAL PARK
Jackson Hole Alliance for Resp. Planning
P.O. Box 2728
Jackson, WY 83001

• Appendix D •
Key Laws and Executive Orders Pertaining to the Management of Parks*

Airport and Airway Development Act of 1970, PL 91-258, 49 USC 1716

American Folklife Preservation Act of 1976, PL 94-201, 89 Stat. 1129, 20 USC 2101-2107

American Indian Religious Freedom Act, PL 95-341, 42 USC 1996

An Act to Improve the Administration of the National Park System, 16 USC 1a7

Antiquities Act of 1906, PL 59-209, 34 Stat. 225, 16 USC 432

Archeological and Historic Preservation Act of 1974, PL 93-291

Archeological Resources Protection Act, PL 96-95, 93 Stat. 712, 16 USC 470aa et seq.

Architectural Barriers Act of 1968, PL 90-480, 82 Stat. 718, 42 USC 4151 et seq.

Bald Eagle and Golden Eagle Protection Act, 16 USC 668

Clean Air Act, as amended; PL 88-206, 42 USC 7401 et seq.

Coastal Zone Management Act of 1972, PL 92-583, 16 USC 1451 et seq.

Concessions Policy Act of 1965, PL 89-249, 16 USC 20 et seq.

Department of Transportation Act of 1966, PL 89-670, 49 USC 1651 et seq.

Disposal of Materials on Public Lands, 30 USC 601-604

Endangered Species Act of 1973, as amended; PL 93-205, 87 Stat. 884, 16 USC 1531 et seq.

Estuary Protection Act, PL 90-454, 16 USC 1221

Executive Order 11593: Protection and Enhancement of the Cultural Environment, 36 FR 8921

Executive Order 11870: Environmental Safeguards on Activities for Animal Damage Control on Federal Lands, 40 FR 30611

Executive Order 11987: Exotic Organisms, 42 FR 26407

Executive Order 11988: Floodplain Management, 42 FR 26951, 3 CFR 121 (Supp 1977)

Executive Order 11989: Off-road Vehicles on Public Lands, 42 FR 26959 and 11644

Executive Order 11990: Protection of Wetlands, 42 fr 26961, 3 CFR 121 (Supp 1977)

Executive Order 11991: Protection and Enhancement of Environmental Quality

Executive Order 12003: Energy Policy and Conservation, 3 CFR 134 (Supp 1977), 42 USC 2601

Executive Order 12088: Federal Compliance with Pollution Control Standards

Executive Order 12372: Intergovernmental Review of Federal Programs, 47 FR 30959

Federal Environmental Pesticide Control Act of 1972, PL 92-516, 7 USC 135 et seq.

Federal Land Policy and Management Act of 1976, PL 94-579, 90 Stat. 2743, as amended; 43 USC 1701 et seq.

Federal Powers Act, 16 USC 823a

Federal Water Pollution Control Act (Clean Water Act), PL 92-500, 33 USC 9 1251 *et seq.*

Federal Water Project Recreation Act, 16 USC 4601-12 to 4601-21

Fish and Wildlife Coordination Act, as amended; PL 85-624, 16 USC 661 *et seq.*

Freedom of Information Act, PL 93-502, 5 USC 552 *et seq.*

General Authorities Act of 1970, as amended; PL 94-458, 16 USC 1a1 *et seq.*

Geothermal Steam Act of 1970, 30 USC 1001-1025

Historic Preservation Act of 1966, PL 89-665, 80 Stat. 915, 16 USC *et seq.*

Historic Sites Act, 44 Stat. 666, 16 USC 461-462

Interagency Consultation to Avoid or Mitigate Adverse Effects on Rivers in the Nation-wide Inventory, 45 FR 59189, 8/15/80, E.S. 80-2

Intergovernmental Coordination Act of 1969, 42 USC 4104, 4231, and 4233

Intergovernmental Cooperation Act of 1968, PL 90-577, 40 USC 4201

Intermodal Surface Transportation and Efficiency Act of 1991, PL 102-240, 105 Stat. 1974

Land and Water Conservation Fund Act of 1965, PL 88-578, 16 USC 4601 *et seq.*

Marine Mammal Protection Act, PL 92-552, 16 USC 1361 *et seq.*

Marine Protection, Research, and Sanctuaries Act of 1972, PL 92-532, 16 USC 1361 *et seq.*

Mining Act of 1872, 30 USC 22

Mining Activity Within National Park Service Areas, PL 94-429, 16 USC 1901 *et seq.*

National Environmental Policy Act of 1969, PL 91-190, 42 USC 4321 *et seq.*

National Historic Preservation Act, PL 89-665, 80 Stat. 915, 16 USC 470 *et seq.*

National Park System Final Procedures for Implementing EO 11988 and 11990 (45 FR 35916 as revised by 47 FR 36718)

National Trails System Act, PL 90-543, 16 USC 1241 to 1249

National Trust Act of 1949, PL 81-408, 63 Stat. 927, 16 USC 468

Noise Control Act of 1972, as amended; PL 92-574, 42 USC 4901 *et seq.*

Payment in Lieu of Taxes Act, PL 94-565, 31 USC 1601 *et seq.*

Resource Conservation and Recovery Act, PL 94-580, 52 USC 6901

The Act of August 25, 1916, National Park Service Organic Act, PL 64-235, 16 USC 1, 2-4, as amended

Wilderness Act of 1964, PL 88-588, 16 USC 1311 *et seq.*

*Adapted from *Vision for the Future: A Framework for Coordination in the Greater Yellowstone Area*

• Appendix E •
National Park Service and National Parks and
Conservation Association Regional Offices

NPS Region	NPS Regional Office	NPCA Regional Office
North Atlantic Region: Connecticut, Maine, Massachusetts, New Hampshire, New Jersey, New York, Rhode Island, Vermont	North Atlantic Region National Park Service 15 State Street Boston, MA 02109 (617) 223-5200	Bruce Craig, Director NPCA Northeast Region 1776 Massachusetts Ave., NW Washington, D.C. 20036 (202) 223-6722
Mid-Atlantic Region: Delaware, Maryland, Pennsylvania, Virginia, West Virginia (excludes parks assigned to the National Capitol Region)	Mid-Atlantic Region National Park Service 143 South Third Street Philadelphia, PA 19106 (715) 597-7013	Bruce Craig, Director NPCA Northeast Region 1776 Massachusetts Ave., NW Washington, D.C. 20036 (202) 223-6722
National Capital Region: Metropolitan area of Washington, D.C., with some units in Maryland, Virginia, West Virginia	National Capital Region National Park Service 1100 Ohio Drive, SW Washington, D.C. 20242 (202) 619-7222	Bruce Craig, Director NPCA Northeast Region 1776 Massachusetts Ave., NW Washington, D.C. 20036 (202) 223-6722
Southeast Region: Alabama, Florida, Georgia, Kentucky, Mississippi, North Carolina, Puerto Rico, South Carolina, Tennessee, the Virgin Islands	Southeast Region National Park Service Richard B. Russell Federal Building 75 Spring Street, SW Atlanta, GA 30303 (404) 331-5185	Don Barger, Director NPCA Southeast Region P.O. Box 105 Norris, TN 37828 (615) 494-9786 (Region also includes Arkansas and Louisiana)
Midwest Region: Illinois, Indiana, Iowa, Kansas, Michigan, Minnesota, Missouri, Nebraska, Ohio, Wisconsin	Midwest Region National Park Service 1709 Jackson Street Omaha, NE 68102 (402) 221-3431	Lori Nelson, Director NCPA Heartland Region 649 Spring Hill Drive Woodbury, MN 55125 (612) 735-8008 (Region also includes North and South Dakota and Oklahoma)
Rocky Mountain Region: Colorado, Montana, North Dakota, South Dakota, Utah, Wyoming	Rocky Mountain Region National Park Service P.O. Box 25287 Denver, CO 80225 (303) 969-2500	Terri Martin, Director NPCA Rocky Mtn. Region Box 1563 Salt Lake City, UT 84110 (801) 532-4796 (Region does not include North and South Dakota)

NPS Region	NPS Regional Office	NPCA Regional Office
Southwest Region: Arizona (northeast corner), Arkansas, Louisiana, New Mexico, Oklahoma, Texas	Western Region National Park Service P.O. Box 728 Santa Fe, NM 87504 (505) 988-6012	Dave Simon 823 Gold Avenue, SW Albuquerque, NM 87102 (505) 247-1221 (Region does not include Arkansas, Oklahoma or Louisiana, but includes all of Arizona)
Western Region: Arizona (most), California, Hawaii, Nevada	Western Region National Park Service 450 Golden Gate Avenue Box 36063 San Francisco, CA 94102 (415) 744-3876	Dale Crane, Director NPCA Pacific NW Region 618 South 223rd Street Des Moines, WA 98198 (206) 824-8808 (Region does not include Arizona or Nevada)
Pacific Northwest Region: Idaho, Oregon, Washington	Pacific Northwest Region National Park Service 83 South King St., Suite 212 Seattle, WA 98104 (206) 553-5565	Dale Crane, Director NPCA Pacific NW Region 618 South 223rd Street Des Moines, WA 98198 (206) 824-8808
Alaska Region: Alaska National Parklands	Alaska Region National Park Service 2525 Gamble Street Anchorage, AK 99503 (907)257-2690	Chip Dennerlein, Director NPCA Alaska Region 329 F Street, Suite 208 Anchorage, AK 99501 (907) 277-6722

Index

Y

Z

Books Building Community

Born out of the 1990 Earth Day celebration is an event that is the cornerstone of a number of environmental programs across America. NPCA's **March for Parks** raises awareness and funds for America's national, state, regional, and local parks by organizing walks and other events around the country. The march has taken a special place as Americans look for ways to take back their heritage, history, and their parks, and to initiate grassroots programs to save their piece of the Earth.

The well-known quote "think globally, act locally" suggests that if each community were to ensure that its particular environment were healthy, that its air and water were clean, that its plant and animal species were thriving under its stewardship, global environmental problems would be minimized. For example, if citizens ensured that factories in their towns did not pollute, nations might not need clean air laws.

On the specific scale of national parks, the same is true. Our parks have been in the hands of those who favor short-term returns over long-term public needs. As a result, many programs—such as planting trees, preserving wildlife habitat, carrying out research, and furthering environmental education—have been given low priority because they produce no immediate commercial or political gain. Therefore, private citizens must step in to ensure that these needed programs become a reality.

Through **March for Parks**, citizens can do just that; take back what is theirs—take back their parks, take back their responsibility. For example, users of Chugach State Park in

Alaska marched to inaugurate a park watch program aimed at taking back their park from criminals engaged in illegal tree-cutting, theft, and vandalism in Chugach. And in Florida, a Miami elementary school teacher marched with her students to raise funds for environmental education materials about Everglades National Park.

March for Parks is more than a march because it reflects the broad mandate of thinking globally and acting locally. Last year, more than 264,000 people across the country raised nearly $1.5 million for park projects. This year we will help more people work to fulfill their local needs, including riverside cleanups, tree planting, recycling programs, and environmental education projects.

March for Parks 1994 had special significance for NPCA because 1994 also marked NPCA's 75th anniversary. In the San Francisco Bay Area, Foghorn Press, publisher of recreation and outdoor books, sponsored a flagship march in our nation's newest national park, the Presidio in San Francisco. **March for Parks 1995** will mark the 25th anniversary of Earth Day on the weekend of April 21, 22 and 23.

Join with individuals nationwide as we work not only to protect our parks, but also to applaud the more than 75 years of citizen action that have created the wonderful National Park System we have today. Each one of us must act locally if we are going to save our parks and save our Earth.

Paul C. Pritchard
President
National Parks and Conservation Association

1776 Massachusetts Avenue N.W., Washington D.C. 20036
Telephone (202) 223-NPCA (6722) / Fax (202) 659-0650